What people are saying about *Business and t.*

"*Business and the Feminine Principle* is a book that is hard to put down because it goes right to the heart: your own heart and the heart of the chaotic changes going on in business today. This is the first book that has given me a completely clear picture of what the feminine side of our nature can mean for business, the world, and my life. You know that every time you turn a page you may be hit with a revelation that expands your thinking: what might business be if the feminine side were opened more fully?"—**Michael Ray**, Stanford University Graduate School of Business, co-author, *Creativity in Business, The Path of the Everyday Hero*, co-editor, *The New Paradigm in Business*

"This author writes with clarity because she sees clearly. What a relief to find a direct and profound understanding of womanhood, rather than a book about women and power. It is a book of awe and hope, not anger; of a veneration of core competencies, both male and female. I believe our organizational world is moving toward psychological and structural states that would benefit from such feminine skills, logics, and responsiveness."— **Dean Berry**, Senior Vice President, Gemini Consulting, author, Master Coach at the Hudson Institute

"As a female entrepreneur, I need to be pushed to think in the abstract, rather than the specific. *Business and the Feminine Principle* performed that much-needed task. The chapter on "diffuse awareness" was especially valuable to me."—**Ann H. Gaither**, Chairperson, The J. H. Heafner Co., Inc.

"*Business and the Feminine Principle* describes not only what is necessary for the transformation of business into a humane and Life nourishing endeavor, but also what is necessary for the survival and evolution of humankind."—**Gary Zukav**, author, *The Dancing Wu Li Masters* and *The Seat of the Soul*

"This very personal and quietly passionate book asks us to explore aspects of human nature that have gone unregarded for too long. We could create so much more together if we would join Carol on this exploration."— **Margaret Wheatley**, author, *Leadership and the New Science* and *A Simpler Way*

"Valuable and fascinating! Carol Frenier reconciles with great clarity and insight specific aspects of feminine psychology and the needs of today's workplace."—**Sally Helgesen**, author, *The Web of Inclusion* and *The Female Advantage: Women's Ways of Leading*

BUSINESS AND THE FEMININE PRINCIPLE

BUSINESS AND THE FEMININE PRINCIPLE

The Untapped Resource

By
CAROL R. FRENIER

Butterworth-Heinemann

Boston Oxford Johannesburg Melbourne New Delhi Singapore

Butterworth-Heinemann
A member of Reed Elsevier group
Copyright © 1997 by Carol R. Frenier

Recognizing the importance of preserving what has been written, Butterworth-Heinemann prints its books on acid-free paper whenever possible.

Library of Congress Cataloging-in-Publication Data
Frenier, Carol R., 1944–
    Business and the feminine principle : the untapped resource / by
Carol R. Frenier.
        p.   cm.
    Includes bibliographical references (p.) and index.
    ISBN 0-7506-9829-2 (pbk. : alk. paper)
    1. Women in business—Psychology. 2. Femininity (Psychology)
3. Corporate culture. I. Title.
    HD6053.F725   1997
    305.43—dc20   96-25638
                                                                 CIP

British Library Cataloguing-in-Publication Data
A catalogue record of this book is available from the British Library.

The publisher offers discounts on bulk orders of this book.

For information, please write:

Manager of Special Sales
Butterworth-Heinemann
313 Washington Street
Newton, MA 02158-1626
Tel: 617-928-2500
Fax: 617-928-2620

For information on all business publications available, contact our World Wide Web home page at: http://www.bh.com

10 9 8 7 6 5 4 3 2 1

Printed in the United States of America

To Bob Frenier—my husband and soul mate—whose radiant masculine energy shines through all of our conversations and who has made both my values and my thinking more accessible to the world.

To Sydney Rice—my coach extraordinaire—who personifies the feminine principle in business better than anyone else I know.

Contents

Preface   xi
Acknowledgments   xvii

1. Introduction   1

PART ONE: THE FEMININE PRINCIPLE   13
  2. Diffuse Awareness   15
  3. The Quick of the Moment   31
  4. Accepting the Cycles of Life   45
  5. Deep Community   61

PART TWO: FEMININE PATTERNS OF WORK   79
  6. Organizing Information and Action   81
  7. Deep Feeling and Radical Trust   95
  8. Mothering and Being Mothered   113
  9. Sensibility about Space   127

PART THREE: FEMININE LEADERSHIP   143
10. Honoring Our Feminine Depths   145
11. Collaboration with the Masculine   163
12. Patterns of Change   179
13. Conclusion   197

References   201

Index   205

Preface

When I graduated from college in June of 1966, I was headed for Washington D.C. to save the world. I had spent the previous summer as an intern at the Peace Corps and had been dazzled by the whirlwind of briefings—on the "Hill," at the State Department, at the Pentagon—that make up the glamorous life of college students in the nation's capital each summer. Still inspired by the youthful Kennedy administration that ended tragically in 1963, I was ready to give my all to Lyndon Johnson's "New Society."

Two and a half years later, I came home to the Boston area to teach high school sociology and American history. I was hired with virtually no teaching credentials, because my social studies chairman wanted people who had some experience in the "real world." As young as I was, my years in Washington D.C. counted as real experience in the world in her view. I spent ten satisfying years in the classroom, "saving the world" in my own way, and I had no thoughts whatsoever of going into business.

But, as fate would have it, I got interested in the film development side of curriculum planning, which led me to a master's degree program in filmmaking at Goddard College's outpost in Cambridge, Massachusetts. From there I joined my husband and two other partners in an enterprise that involved running a cable television program. In order to pay ourselves, we had to sell advertising and produce the commercial spots along with the program. Thus my entry into business. From producing that cable television program, we moved on to broadcast advertising, because our local clients wanted to try that medium. We hired staff and developed a specialty in regional radio and television advertising, eventually focusing on dairy accounts, that is, dairy producers, those companies whose milk you buy in paper cartons or half-gallon plastic jugs.

This was not my idea of saving the world. I had envisioned making films about important social issues, and here I was learning the basics of accounting, dealing with banks and lawyers, deciding whom to hire, and managing people as they came onboard. But I found I loved the camaraderie, and I was surprised at the decency and honesty I found among the small vendors from whom I bought supplies and services. I came to think of this "street economy" in which I was enmeshed as fundamentally different from the corporate economy for which I still had so much disdain. (We were not yet incorporated.) I kept saying that I had no idea why I was in business, but that someday I would understand why I was acquiring these skills that were seemingly irrelevant to my "real" career.

Sixteen years later, my husband and I are still in business. We reached our peak, in terms of size, in the late 1980s when we had ten employees and worked in twenty different markets. Now we are back to just the two of us. After all we tried, we found we preferred to be small.

Concurrent with developing the business, at some point in the early 1980s I read Carl Jung's autobiography, *Memories, Dreams, Reflections*. I did not truly recognize at the time how profoundly this book had changed my life, but it was the start of a long journey into my psyche. The richest part of this journey was the exploration of the archetypal feminine, that is, those mysterious sacred images of the feminine that go far beyond the specific traits and roles we ascribe to the feminine in our day-to-day lives. By day I would struggle with the realities of budgets, personality conflicts, and demanding clients. At night, I would read Esther Harding, Marion Woodman, and Marie Louise von Franz.

These seemingly opposite activities—developing a business and reading Jungian depth psychology—were really deeply connected. Business is the distribution of goods and services and all the complicated relationships among people and materials that make such distribution possible. It is not ancillary to life, but one of life's primary channels. To be outside of that activity, being the introverted student that I am, I might have missed much of life altogether. Now that life had my attention through my practical business activity, I began to struggle in a concrete way with the implications of what I was reading. What was the purpose of life? What human systems really worked? What human behavior served life? What did people need to be productive and fulfilled, and were these requirements different for men than for women? And so much more.

As we incorporated and gained more staff, I became president and the primary manager of the people in our company. I needed to learn as much as I could about effective working relationships. I noticed early on that I viewed these relationships differently from my male partners. Many of our female employees, who made up the bulk of our staff, viewed relationships as I did. We were all sufficiently good friends—men and women together, operating in an intense environment but with no rigid rules—that the dynamics of male-female relationships were out in the open. That openness might have been a corporate manager's nightmare, but it was real life to us. We did not plan our business that way. We just grew so organically that our business structure reflected our private lives far more than it would have had we started with the prevailing ideas about how a business should operate.

Adding to the diversity at the office was the fact that some of the men had strong feminine traits just as some of the women had strong masculine traits. That fact alone would have shifted my exploration from male-female relationships to masculine-feminine relationships, had I not already been drawn to that dichotomy by my Jungian reading, which led me to see that each of us has both masculine and feminine components to our psyche.

During the 1980s I also became concerned with the long-term health of the environment. I began to see a relationship between what was missing in our treatment of the earth and qualities of the feminine that I did not see getting much attention in our business culture. With a sense of increasing futility I watched endless proposals being made about how to respond to our ecological crisis. Something at the heart of the matter was still unspoken.

As I became more and more preoccupied with these issues, I started to work on distilling my understanding of what the archetypal feminine actually *is*, and what it can contribute to business and to public life in general. This book offers my best understanding of this subject. I have tried to put this material into language that is understandable for everyday life and especially for the workplace.

The archetypal feminine, once again, includes those mysterious and sacred images of the feminine that go far beyond the specific traits and roles we ascribe to the feminine in our day-to-day lives. Because these images are preexistent in the human psyche, they find their way into myths, legends, and fairy tales. Archetypes by their very nature are unlimited. They open us to a greater understanding of universal themes that are beyond human comprehension in their entirety—masculine and feminine, the warrior and the hero, the virgin and the crone. Stereotypes, on the other hand, reduce the content of these larger images to prescribed behavior patterns. The feminine as archetype—what I am calling the feminine principle—can be gleaned from mythology and from our own intuition and experiences.

In Part 1 I describe four aspects of this feminine principle as I see it. The categories are mine in the sense that I organized them according to my own observations and experiences. But in a larger sense, they belong to the whole field of Jungian depth psychology and beyond, because I have drawn on myths and the works of countless men and women who have observed masculine and feminine qualities throughout the ages.

Diffuse awareness is a concept discussed in great detail by Irene Claremont de Castillejo in *Knowing Woman: A Feminine Psychology*, first published in the United States in 1973, but developed somewhat earlier. *The quick of the moment* comes from a quote from Robert Stein's *Incest and Human Love*; this concept describes a feminine quality that has been touched on by many authors in more complex fashion, particularly by Marion Woodman. *Accepting the cycles of life* is an idea that is written about so widely that it would be impossible to attribute it to any given author. And although *deep community* is my own phrase, my thinking about community draws heavily on the writings of Scott Peck and my participation in his and other community-building workshops.

In Part 2 I describe some patterns of behavior that I have observed in myself and in other women in the workplace that seem to be congruent with the feminine principle. I hope that these patterns will give the reader a more concrete understanding of the concepts I describe in Part 1.

Part 3 explores some of my thoughts on what constitutes feminine leadership, that is, what we need to do to bring the feminine principle into the workplace, as opposed to how women might assume power within existing structures.

Examining feminine leadership in light of the feminine principle, as opposed to taking the stand that women need to find positions of power, is important. This is not just a book for women. The human feminine consciousness I describe may be experienced by more women than men, but women do not experience the feminine exclusively. There will be some men for whom the ideas in this book will be very familiar and some women for whom the ideas will be very foreign. There is masculine and feminine in all of us in some proportion, but that exact proportion varies widely from person to person. I have occasionally used the words "women" and "men" to describe what I really mean as personalities with more highly developed feminine consciousness versus those with a more highly developed masculine consciousness, because I find it simply too awkward to do otherwise. But I hope each reader will include him- or herself wherever appropriate, regardless of the language.

As I describe in more detail throughout this book, I believe we are facing turbulent times in which the human species will be put to a difficult test. I believe we will need to find new ways to organize our relationships with each other and with the earth. I hope that both men and women will find contained in this text information and insights about the feminine principle that will spark new and broader thinking for the future.

Acknowledgments

A book is created from a lifetime of learning—from books, from conversations with people, from life experiences. I will never know where this book really began or how many people or places have contributed to its final form. But I would like to thank the following people and communities for their inspiration and support:

The grand dames of Jungian depth psychology: Marie Louise von Franz and Marion Woodman, whose books awakened my feminine psyche, and Chessie Stevenson, who took me deep into my own dreams.

My friends and spiritual companions for over a decade: Susan and Allan Anderson, Linda Atkins and David Blocher, Art and Barbara Smith, Colquitt Meacham and David Brockway, Susan Hamilton, and Linda and Bill Mueffelmann.

The people of Beyond War, now the Foundation for Global Community, who modeled for me what it meant to put the earth first.

My World Business Academy network of fellow travelers: Barbara Shipka, Jeanne Borei, John Pehrson, Jacqui Cambata, Jan Nickerson and John Graham, Anne and Tom Rarich, Susan Miller, Ganson Taggart, Manny Elkind, Terry Mollner, Juli Ann Reynolds, Patricia Stimpson, John and Bunny Thompson, Anne

Hyde, Jim Schwarz, Linda Morris, Herman and Julie Maynard, Bob and Pamela Mang, Gary Zukav, Pat Barrentine, John Renesch, and all the others too numerous to mention.

The First Branch Valley towns of Tunbridge and Chelsea, Vermont, whose physical beauty and richly connected human communities have been the womb within which I could think and write.

My two families of origin: parents and siblings, and especially my nieces and nephews, who make me laugh out loud and remind me why the long-term health of the earth matters.

And finally, Karen Speerstra, publishing director of the U.S. Business Books series at Butterworth-Heinemann, for her intelligent and gracious midwifing of so many new ideas.

Chapter 1

Introduction

Humpty Dumpty sat on a wall,
Humpty Dumpty had a great fall.
All the king's horses,
And all the king's men,
Couldn't put Humpty together again.

The earth we live on is looking more and more like a cracked egg all the time, and the rhyme from our childhood about Humpty Dumpty can express very well our despair about putting it back together. All the king's horses and all the king's men—all the well-meaning scientists, politicians, public servants, and business people, and especially our vast military power—have made very little progress in putting our Humpty Dumpty world back together again. But within the rhyme itself is an interesting clue pointing us to a possible solution. All the king's horses and all the king's men were unsuccessful, but did anyone think to consult the queen?

I am excited about the dialogue that is currently taking place about the impact of so many women in the workplace—at executive managerial levels, not just at the bottom of the ladder. We are beginning to become conscious that women bring certain qualities into professional life, even if we think of these qualities only in the limited form of the softer qualities of employee comfort and consensus building. The presence of feminine energy, some will argue, increases creativity as well as making the work environment more congenial.

But neither the congeniality nor the enhanced creativity of women in the workplace are enough to explain why I have been so obsessed over the past decade with understanding the essential difference between masculine and feminine energy. When I rediscovered the Humpty Dumpty rhyme, I finally realized that, in my mind, the integration of feminine energy into the public sphere may be critical to our survival and evolution as a species. More than being nice, it may be absolutely necessary, and that changes the importance of the work that we are called upon to do. "Women's work," once a catchphrase for all work that was demeaning and unimportant—and the source of some of women's deepest wounds and low self-esteem—is a phrase we may now have to reclaim and elevate to a sacred level.

Sam Keen wrote an interesting comment on women in public life in *Creation Magazine*:

> In the degree that women have recently entered into the public world of business and government and have begun to define themselves as competitors and executives, they have started to take on many of the personality characteristics (and diseases of stress) of the warrior. But to date, they have remained innocent of the single most important defining activity of the warrior— the systematic education in violence and the willingness to kill. Short of entering fully into the power-violence-killing game, women will not gain equal political and economic power with men and the traditional psychological structure will remain. (Keen 1987, p. 10)

I was surprised by how totally I agreed with this statement. After spending sixteen years in business, I acknowledge that I do not inherently feel the capacity to be a warrior. A lot of men I know are asking the question What do I want to be a warrior *for*? Or *Do*

I want to be one? But few of them seem to doubt their capacity. I do doubt mine.

On the other hand, I think I have a lot to say about what the warring should be *for*, when it is appropriate, and when it needs to stop. If women—and men—who feel the same as I do can get past the painful question: Is there something missing in me that warriors have? they might get to the much more exciting question: Is there something in me that is not yet fully expressed that might contribute to the whole?

Keen's statement is true only if public life is exclusively defined by the warrior system. When I think of the warrior system, I also think of the hunter, which, though not identical with the warrior, possesses a similar capacity, and willingness to kill. The hunter of prehistoric times is often contrasted with the gatherer, which we think of as a more feminine role. I am asking myself specifically, What is the role of the feminine in public life today? and I am looking for something like a modern version of "gathering," as a component of life equal in stature to, and capable of balancing, "hunting" and "warring." Keen also wrote:

> I don't know if any woman can understand the incredible sadness and sorrow of what the male had done to himself. Even in his most peaceful imagination, the only image of peace he can bring up is a picture of a woman and child. We have in our deepest consciousness no male image of peace. That is what warfare has done to us. (Keen 1987, p. 11)

I sense that the human species as a whole is craving such a conscious image of peace to guide our public as well as our private lives. For two thousand years we have developed and perfected hunting and warring skills, honing in on the prey and understanding the mechanical aspects of our universe so we can control it. Something else is needed to make life work. This something else is not a substitute for the hunter-warrior consciousness; it is a partner.

PSYCHE AND EROS

In the ancient Greek myth about Psyche and Eros, Eros flees from Psyche after, against his wishes, she shines a light on him to discover his beauty. Psyche goes to his jealous mother, the goddess Aphrodite, for help in getting him back and is assigned four grueling tasks, which have been interpreted psychologically as initiations into feminine mastery. Psyche's first task is to sort a hopelessly huge mound of seeds before daybreak. There is no logical way that she can do this within the time frame given. But some ants, symbols of her feminine instincts, come out to help her. Somehow the ants are able to sort through the confusion of the masses of seeds (Neumann 1990).

Some days in the masculine world of business, I feel exactly like Psyche. The task I feel compelled to perform seems utterly impossible. I know that there is something else that needs to be said and done, but I cannot formulate it, certainly not in the rushed time frame of a business meeting with a crammed agenda.

My friend Susan Anderson once said to me that men have taught women how to think the way men think, but women have not succeeded in teaching men to think the way women think. This is not the fault of either men or women. The difficulty in communicating how women think is inherent in the nature of feminine consciousness, the strength and value of which comes from the depths, not from the visible heights. That is why masculine consciousness is so often associated with sunlight, and the feminine with moonlight. Remember that in the moonlight you can see other light sources, but in the sunlight, it is very difficult to do so. So the rational, well-organized masculine patterns of thought shine so brightly in our day-to-day business life—make such logical sense—that women, and men who are drawn to the feminine, hesitate to question them. It is hard to hold onto our inner depths in the light of day.

But since Psyche was successful in using her feminine instincts to sift through the masculine seeds and order them, there is hope that we too can become conscious of our own feminine processes and acquire confidence in their value. This ability to sort the seemingly impossible mound of seeds of our present-day global dilemmas may be what the feminine principle has to offer us as we work together to put our Humpty Dumpty world back together again.

ALL THE GOOD THINGS WE'VE GOT

This is not a book about what's wrong with men or patriarchy. I have watched my husband wince each time the p-word is used, and have finally decided to drop it from my vocabulary. It had already served its purpose for me, and now it only causes pain. In his mind, blaming the patriarchy means that all that is wrong with the world is blamed on men and men's systems, and no acknowledgment is given to what men have done right or how women have contributed to the current state of affairs.

A lot *has* been done right. One of the central qualities of masculinity is focused consciousness (Claremont de Castillejo 1973). If you are one sperm among millions, you have to pay attention in a very focused way to get to the ovum. And you have to have courage, determination, and a willingness to act. The same is true for hunting, for protecting one's turf or nation in war, or for building a technology that has made it possible for me to talk by modem to friends in Australia.

Focused consciousness means being able to separate and distinguish one thing from another, including one's own individuality from that of the group, and to be able to build something using information and ideas. As it separates one thing from another, focused consciousness has a natural tendency toward hierarchical ordering, because it sees the inherent qualities or lack thereof in each object. Such thinking has produced not only technologies for living, but philosophies, religions, and abstract thinking. These in turn have created a legal, contractual system that has produced the most effective system of justice we have ever known, its shortcomings notwithstanding. Focused consciousness has also created an environment supportive of new ideas, creativity, and a kind of uniform, rational civility. Although focused consciousness has a tendency toward promiscuity—generativity run amuck—it also places a high value on restraint, which we can see in all the world's most lasting spiritual systems.

Women wouldn't *really* want to give up the capacity for focused consciousness, not even in themselves, let alone in men. Along with our Constitution and our freedom of speech, we are all accustomed to our beautiful machines—machines for playing music and monitoring the heart, machines for sewing and cooking, driving and flying, communicating and sorting information. We like having efficient systems of food distribution, and we like our modern homes—indoor plumbing in particular. And I, personally, would protect a skilled and honest auto mechanic with my life, not to mention a Federal Express driver who can make it up my icy hill in January.

In fact, the true masculine and true feminine are deeply in love with each other, even as they are also caught in a dynamic tension that is born of their differences. I have sometimes looked across a conference room or a board meeting and been in love with all the men at once. Sometimes we forget that it is our very differences that attract us so strongly to each other. That is the design of nature. Otherwise we would never engage long enough with each other to produce a child, literally or figuratively.

WHAT'S MISSING

So, what, then, is missing? For all the good things we've got, we are also trapped in an economy that is driven by the production of material goods, not value. How *much* an individual company can produce and sell to generate how much profit to shareholders is more important than what a company's products contribute to life. Even when we are providing a service, our work is characterized by a frenetic drive to convince people that they need what we have to offer. Our systems are not primarily based on producing things that will be truly useful, but more often on what we want, which is more accurately what our advertising culture has taught us to want. That leaves most of us in a position of earning our living producing things that have no real meaning or utility in life. We don't choose this work consciously; we are adrift in our economic system, like ice floes in the spring thaw.

There are other problems as well. Several years ago a fifty-year-old white male banker I know was laid off. An Estonian refugee, he had found his way into the American Dream by acquiring a degree from Brown University and building a successful banking career. Since his layoff, he has done everything from baking to painting. Despite all his efforts, he has lost his home and has not been able to earn a living at anywhere near the level of his ability.

Recently I also found myself in an awkward financial position. A large client went bankrupt leaving me holding a five-figure receivable I couldn't collect. This happened right in the middle of a bad business cycle. I hunkered down and took as little money out of the company as I could until times got better. Then, when I tried to refinance my house to absorb the loss— thus offering my own equity as the solution to the problem—I was told I did not have the income stream to support the larger mortgage.

I do not conclude from either of these situations that our system is callous. A business that is not generating enough income has to lay off employees, no matter how loyal. The institution that refused to remortgage my house made a safe decision based on statistics. But still something important is missing. Like the banker who was laid off, I had my first harsh experience of being up against circumstances that my best efforts could not control, and I discovered how much discomfort I felt about asking my friends or family for help. How much worse this must be for the truly down and out.

I do not, frankly, look to politics for an answer to this problem. Social welfare programs administered by rational bureaucracies do not offer the spontaneous response that I am looking for. There are better examples in our daily lives for how we could work with each other in the ways that I am imagining. When we actually come into contact with each other and live our daily lives side by side, there is a remarkable amount of automatic connectivity and support. On a street corner, we greet each other. We give directions, warn strangers of danger, and look out for the children and the elderly spontaneously. This is the undercurrent of life—what I would call the domain of the archetypal feminine—that we are shocked to find missing when a violent act occurs in our orbit. We have no name for this undercurrent, but it is there as solid as life itself.

I am trying to feel my way into this living undercurrent, to become conscious of what the patterns are there, and to replicate them in the workplace. Imagine a group of people coming out the door of a store, for example. One carries a large bag. As this person approaches the door, two others automatically reach out to hold the door for the one whose hands are occupied. They nod acknowledgment to each other. Then someone lets the door go in such a way that it will not swing back and hit someone else. All this occurs in seconds with barely any thought, and all the players go on about their way.

As crazy as this may seem, this is how I would *really* like our economic life to be. I crave the opportunity to give my work to the world without constantly having to think about winning or losing or making enough money at it. I would like to know that if I go down one path and it doesn't produce results, that someone will, figuratively, hold the door for me while I figure out another avenue to try. I would like to feel secure enough about this to freely hold the door for someone else in the same circumstances; but not being sure that the door will be held for me, I am self-absorbed in figuring out how to manage everything for myself. I have often thought that the real motivation behind hoarding, and a lack of generosity in general, is not greed but fear—fear that someday we will not be able to provide for ourselves and no one will be there for us if we fail. Having worked with some very wealthy clients, I know that having a lot of money doesn't help much with this fear. What we think we need is very relative, and the wealthy are sometimes the most fearful of abandonment, which is perhaps the reason why they have been driven to hoard so much.

Something *is* missing in our economic life, and it is not the lack of independence and motivation that the conservative thinkers fear, nor the lack of generosity that the liberal thinkers fear. It is as if there is a missing piece that has not yet presented itself in our line of vision.

DIVERGING AND CONVERGING

On a Sunday night closest to Valentine's Day, our local country church hosted game night to brighten up the long, cold winter in Vermont. Everyone brought cookies and a favorite game. On this particular night, before we got started on other games, there was something else that captured our attention. Someone had brought a copy of a book called *Magic Eye* (NE Thing Enterprises 1993). This book is a series of color designs. You hold a picture close to your eyes, let your eyes relax, and then slowly draw the page away from you. If you do it right, you will see a three-dimensional picture. Someone across the room got it and squealed with pleasure as multicolored fish suspended themselves shimmering in three-dimensional water in front of her.

The trick is to let your eyes diverge, which means that they move in different directions or branch out from a common point. Just the opposite of focusing, your eyes actually look to a point *beyond* the object in this exercise, thus picking up the third dimension, which focusing cannot produce. You can only do this if you let your eyes *really* relax. Thinking about it won't help. You will only know how to do it when you do it. As soon as you move the page quickly, or consciously focus your eyes, you will lose the three-dimensional image. Eventually you can get the hang of going back and forth between focusing and diverging.

This simple game provides a good analogy for the kind of feminine perception that is outside the frame of our highly developed masculine focused consciousness. Diverging your eyes is not hard to do, but before you succeed in doing it, the capability doesn't exist for you at all. The invisibility of this kind of perceiving to those who have not experienced it may explain why we have taken so long to consider how this capability might help us solve what look like our most unsolvable problems.

Since the purpose of this book is to illuminate the feminine principle, the book is written in a style that is congruent with feminine perceptions and patterns of thought. Some readers will feel at home with this style; others may have to work harder to set aside a lifelong practice of analyzing a focused idea quickly instead of allowing their minds to play with a diffuse image that might provide a fuller understanding of what I am trying to describe. For the reader more oriented toward masculine focused consciousness I hope there will be a benefit to "staying with" this feminine style despite some difficulty. The thinking presented will not always be linear, and it may, from time to time, appear to be contradictory. There is, however, a very fine line between contradiction and paradox, and accepting paradox, as you will soon see, is an integral part of the feminine principle.

For those women—and men—who naturally favor feminine patterns of perceiving and thinking, I hope the next four chapters describing various aspects of the feminine principle will be an affirmation. For those men and women in whom masculine focused consciousness is more highly developed, I hope these chapters will help illuminate what the feminine has to offer to public life.

To affirm and illuminate what the feminine has to offer in no way diminishes what masculine consciousness offers. A mature man with strong focused consciousness skills, who knows his own ground and is on his true path in the service of life, acts, it seems to me, with stunning grace and power in the world. Matthew Fox's work *Original Blessing* and Wendell Berry's *In Memory of Old Jack* are two wonderful examples from the intellectual and literary worlds. Paul Hawken's *The Ecology of Commerce* and the consulting work he does in the field are examples from business. What I call the radiant masculine—the capacity to shine a light like a laser beam on the heart of the matter and stand for that truth—continues to be important in the world. But men's work and women's work, or more precisely, masculine and feminine work, are needed together to accomplish the essential task of generating new life. To go back to the metaphor of human sexuality, neither a sperm nor an ovum alone can conceive a child.

Part I

The Feminine Principle

Chapter 2

Diffuse Awareness

I cannot stress too strongly that . . . diffuse awareness . . . is emphatically *not unc*onscious. Its difference in quality from masculine focused consciousness . . . lies in its whole unbroken state which defies scientific analysis and logical deduction, and is therefore not possible to formulate in clear unambiguous terms.

—IRENE CLAREMONT DE CASTILLEJO, *Knowing Woman: A Feminine Psychology*

Irene Claremont de Castillejo used the phrases "focused consciousness" and "diffuse awareness" to distinguish between two levels of awareness that exist in some proportion in all of us. Focused consciousness we know well; it is the basis of our culture and our educational systems. Diffuse awareness is far less understood or appreciated. Yet, as Claremont de Castillejo points out, diffuse awareness is something "most children are born with and many women retain" (Claremont de Castillejo 1973, 15). Diffuse awareness is a specific feminine capacity of the mind equivalent in power and importance to masculine focused consciousness. In this chapter I look at what diffuse awareness is, how it operates in life, and why it is an important tool in our business lives.

What is diffuse awareness? Let's look back to the *Magic Eye* exercise as an analogy. Diffuse awareness requires the same kind of divergence mentally that the *Magic Eye* exercise requires of your eyes. In the eye exercise, you look beyond the object in an unfocused way. This allows you to take in the third dimension, altering the relatedness between the different pieces of the picture. What you see is a field rather than a series of points. Diffuse awareness involves perceiving reality in the same way, constantly seeing the complex relationships between things as an important piece of information in itself.

A mother caring for small children offers an example of how diffuse awareness works in the world. Fathers do this too, but I have watched more fathers than mothers go crazy trying to organize the activity of small children to some purpose. Most mothers don't seem to feel the same need for order, or maybe they simply give up trying to organize children twenty-four hours a day. The critical task is to keep the children alive, interested, and, preferably, happy. This can happen in many satisfactory ways. Instead of specifically directing the child, the mother uses her energy to keep the child moving in a life-enhancing direction, out of harm's way, but that is about all she can do most of the time. Which is fine, because there are many positive paths for the child to take in the course of a day. Playing ball or being deep in a fantasy are not inherently more or less important than examining a frog. There is time for everything and no need for a plan in the imaginal life of the child. This process is not unlike the cells of the body dividing as the body grows physically, each cell growing according to its own requirements. Interestingly, though, the cells are all inextricably linked to the larger processes—the intake of oxygen and the flow of the blood.

Through her diffuse awareness, the mother keeps in tune with everything that touches the life of the child. The database is enormous, including conflicting and paradoxical information. Grasping everything that affects her child's life, in all its diversity and with all its contradictions, is the essence of her work, whether or not she can report verbally what she is perceiving. As if working on a puzzle, she takes in all the pieces through diffuse awareness and processes them to reveal a total picture. One piece is not necessarily more important than another; conversely, the puzzle is not complete if even one piece is missing.

Feminine diffuse awareness, then, takes in *everything*. Whereas the masculine energy focuses well on generating a *new* reality; the feminine perceives more clearly all of what is real right now, including what is not likely to go away no matter how much we would like it to disappear. As we shall see, this aspect of feminine awareness has powerful implications for business.

THE GARDEN

Before we look at its potential impact on business, I want to give you one more example of how diffuse awareness works in ordinary life. I have always loved planting but have never had enough land to do very much of it. When I moved to Vermont, I suddenly had the opportunity to work a 1,200-square-foot vegetable garden. Tending to this garden daily opened me up to a conscious experience of effectively relying on my capacity for diffuse awareness. But I did not understand this immediately by any means. I want to take you through the evolution of my thinking about the garden, so you can see how differently I approached it at the end than at the beginning.

First of all, it was a miracle to me that I had all that space to plant. I poured over my gardening books and mapped out what would go where. I was religious about composting, adding each banana peel to my compost pile with a pleasure I cannot possibly convey. All winter long I thought about the nutrients I would be adding to the soil in the spring.

I have long taken easily to companion planting, which means side-by-side planting of seedlings that will enhance each other's growth and repel each other's diseases or pests. I plant the all-purpose repellents—garlic, onions, nasturtiums, and marigolds—around the periphery of my garden and along the paths. Not only do I have little trouble with animals and bugs, but in August my garden is gorgeous in all shades of yellow, orange, and red. Originally I planned an herb garden, but then I found that the herbs were much too valuable scattered throughout the garden to segregate in one place.

For my first two summers, I was in ecstasy over every development. First there was the broccoli, then the beets, then the beans and potatoes, then the tomatoes, then the squash and the pumpkins, and, finally, the brussels sprouts well after the first frost. Along about the second week in August, everything merged together into a mass of lushness obliterating the paths. I took countless pictures from every direction.

Then I became aware of perennial flowers. In the first year, under the passionate tutelage of my youngest sister, Arlene, I planted a euphorbia, a dianthus, and a coreopsis, all plant names I had never even heard of before. I also acquired a bleeding heart, a Shasta daisy, and a purple Michaelmas daisy. Bit by bit I added more. At some point in the beginning of that second summer, it occurred to me that the steep slope in front of my house might be an ideal site for a perennial meadow. It was in full sun and was a nuisance to mow. It took me all summer to dig and prepare those beds and to transplant a few items there.

By March heading into my third season, I was in a frenzy of planning. I had every garden catalog available, I had mapped out every bed, and I had placed my orders for plants. The snow had barely left the hill in April when I was out there rearranging and planting according to my map. And then it started to bloom. What an extraordinary thing that something so small and dormant can erupt into something so graceful and alive! The euphorbia turned brilliant yellow. The tulips came up deep red. The "Six Hills Giant" nepeta arched its delicate spikes to the sky and exploded in dainty blue flowers.

No sooner had things started to bloom than I started to see things placed differently. The local garden experts laughed at me and said, "So what else is new?" Change, I had not yet learned, was the way of life for a flower gardener. Vegetables get rotated, to be sure, but the flowers can be rearranged endlessly. I got out my notebook and started drawing maps again; then I revised them, afraid I would forget each idea if I didn't write it down.

I had already grasped the notion of height and color. The tall ones go in the back, and you place the colors in ways that please you. In the third summer I started to notice texture and scale. Some things just look right together; others don't. A plant seen from a distance needs to be large and can be mangy, I discovered; a plant close up on the path where I am walking can be less striking, but needs to be exquisite in detail.

By the end of that summer I noticed that I was no longer mapping. I had stopped thinking conceptually about my garden. Instead of having to draw it to imagine what the whole would look like, I would just walk by something and sense where it should be. The real pleasure came from putting my hands in the soil and moving things in the moment.

In a few cases I moved things in full bloom, not a good idea generally, but it felt right at the time because small, delicate things were being swamped by large, dramatic things, neither to good advantage. As I planted one plant I saw a way to plant bulbs around it so they would be seen first, then camouflaged when the plant came in later. This awareness seemed to come to me, not at all like an active idea, but as a direct communication from my eyes to my brain.

Veteran perennial gardeners know all of this, I'm sure, and much more that I haven't had the pleasure of discovering yet. But to me, at age fifty, it was a revelation that you could wander around and work your flower beds by feel. I don't know where the information is coming from when I get the urge to move a plant from one place to another. I am still not used to trusting my hands to be instruments of something that feels more instinctual than mental. If I can't specifically think it, I have trouble believing it is real.

When I talk about working my flower beds by feel, then, I really mean that I am relying on my diffuse awareness. I am allowing all the peripheral information to come in and inform my decision even if I cannot tell you how I know what I know. This is similar to, but not exactly the same as, intuition, which is more like having a hunch about something that you can often describe later in conceptual terms. Diffuse awareness has more to do with the breadth and scope of information that you can take in simultaneously and that may be too complex to reduce to a concept.

One of the big surprises for me in allowing myself to rely on my diffuse awareness was how *alive* it made me feel, and I would like to have a lot more of this aliveness in my life. I can only draw the analogy of eating an extraordinary piece of food that is so unexpected that it startles and delights the tastebuds. You don't need to be invited back for a second piece, nor do you need to explain why you are doing so. This feeling of aliveness that I get from my garden makes me suspect that it is important to value my diffuse awareness in all aspects of my life.

USING DIFFUSE AWARENESS AT WORK

The lack of public recognition of diffuse awareness as a real skill, and the difficulty we have in explaining how we know what we know thanks to this process, is a big part of what stops us from consciously bringing this enormous feminine capacity for perception into our business lives. Unconsciously, I have used my diffuse awareness in business all along, and I am certain that other women and men do the same thing. As I built my company, my primary work was financial planning and task management; I did cash flow and accrual projections and managed the people servicing the clients. Consultants helped me formulate organizational and workflow charts, all of which I understood and used, but the truth is I didn't have as much faith in them as I did in the information that I took in as I talked to people and observed them in action. I could usually feel it if a project was working or if it wasn't. I knew when someone was upset or when someone was struggling. So although I certainly used the charts, projections, and business plans, which I could explain, the peripheral data was at least as important to my sense of the well-being of my business. One evening a board member arrived early for a meeting and commented on the fact that there was an ambience in our office that really worked, which he could not name, but which he knew I had created. It was one of my first clues that I was doing something right in my business, something that was outside of the usual measuring systems.

The ambience that really worked had to do with the comfort level of the people in my office. They were not always at peace, as you will soon see, but their relationships with each other were real enough that everyone could feel at home. The creation of such ambience is often linked to women, because it is their diffuse awareness that takes in the nuances of human relationships as vital information in the environment. One company principal commented that his women managers are "more willing to sit and talk about issues in order to come to consensus." The men, he said, "drive through with more of a charge." The women are "very clearly more concerned with their people." Women, he feels, are better at process; men are better at decisive action. Similarly, a male senior manager observed, "Women seem much more adept at group process than men: the early 'relating' stages, the later discussion/decision-making stages, and the follow-up steps to ensure continued alignment."

This is not new information. It has become almost a cliché to say that women generally do better at consensus building and dialogue than men. But this is not the only area of business activity that can be positively affected by the fact that feminine antennae are always out. When Elaine Reilly was a manager at a high-tech company in the early 1980s, she was assigned a task that seemed almost invisible to everyone else. A group of data-entry clerks, to whom nobody was paying any attention, was notorious for inaccurate work. Down the line it took a lot of time to correct the data, and, even with that effort, there was constant doubt about the accuracy of the data. Elaine was asked to take this group on.

First she brought in some strong managers. She assessed the situation and found that the group had the data and the technology to do the job, but they had no visibility, no personal development, and no sense of business partnership with their customers. So she started to work on the people. A born teacher, she explained how the data was used and what kind of impact it had on the marketplace. She got people to take ownership not only of their own data, but of everyone's data that was part of the wider system. One of her first activities was to define with her managers a competency model for this unique work. They assessed the sixty employees and developed a process by which the employees defined their own development plan as part of their work goals. Elaine was convinced that if people consciously developed their own skills and business acumen, the goals would take care of themselves.

Simultaneously she worked with the businesspeople who were her customers. She got them to pay more attention to what kind of data they were using and how their information systems affected policy decisions within their own business units. And she got them to be aware of the cause-and-effect relationships with the larger data field in their industry, just as she had gotten her own employees to do. At a time when it was unusual to have a meeting to discuss data collection even within her company, Elaine's mind was attuned to the possible uses of a worldwide information system that would benefit everyone in her industry. Before she was done, she was linked with a prestigious university whose staff wanted opportunities for master's students to work with the system.

When I talked to Elaine about this process, it was clear that right from the beginning she had been interested in the whole data management picture—far beyond her own company, or even her customers. But despite her ability to talk about it in great detail now, I would wager that when she first started the project she was feeling her way into it much as I had done with my garden. Eventually she developed an architecture for data management totally unlike any others because it was based on the roles and responsibilities of people concerning the creating, storing, and use of the data. In her architecture she identified four major groups who had a stake in the system. The first group provided the data itself; they were the people from whom the raw data came. The second group used the data. The third group, like her own people, acted as custodians for the data. The fourth group included the data controllers, that is, those business managers who made policy decisions about how the data was defined. Then she developed service contracts between all four groups so that all of their needs could be met—establishing work goals and development plans, in a sense, for her clients as she had done with her employees.

Elaine's approach to her task offers a good example of the breadth of diffuse awareness and also its essential difference from intuition. Intuition gives us a holistic picture that comes from within; it is a gut feeling, as opposed to the data that we get directly through our senses of seeing, hearing, tasting, smelling, and touching. But intuition is not necessarily as comprehensive as diffuse awareness, nor as attuned to relatedness; and diffuse awareness uses both sensate and intuitive skills to take in information from the environment. Elaine, by her own definition, is best at painting a big picture and making models simple enough so that people can understand some very complex systems and ideas. But there is no doubt in my mind that she would not have succeeded without an extraordinary ability to absorb and keep track of many critical, sensate details. Five years were invested in this effort, she reports, during which time she kept "two sets of books." The first set of books reported to management how improvements in data quality improved business performance, that is, increased revenues and reduced costs and people. In the second set of books she recorded the effort to develop employees and clients as a kind of "clandestine activity."

"*BOTH* BOTH-AND *AND* EITHER-OR"

Diffuse awareness does not edit. It takes in data whether or not that data fits our definitions of what is the proper domain of our company, our industry, or even business in general. The ambience in an office, for example, includes the internal states of people and the emotional affects of situations—which at best confuse and often greatly discomfort businesspeople. This subtle information comes at us from all directions, as it certainly did for Elaine, if we are allowing our diffuse awareness to work.

Some people have used the phrase "both-and" to distinguish a mind-set that validates different kinds of information, as opposed to what they perceive as the dominant "either-or" mentality in business today. This distinction helps us understand that we can value two different types of tasks or two different types of people at once, but viewed simply, it can actually keep us in the mind-set of contrasts. We actually end up choosing "*either* both-and *or* either-or." For example, if we are valuing "both-and" as a mind-set, then the people who make judgments in favor of an inclusive organization are seen as more enlightened than the people who prefer an organization that is more hierarchically structured. In its most mature—and complex—form, diffuse awareness is a "*both* both-and *and* either-or" mind-set, because diffuse awareness paradoxically takes in both inclusivity and exclusivity as valid sources of data in the environment. This simultaneous processing requires an ability to live with paradox. Paradox is extremely difficult for the human mind because it means accepting that something is true even though it clearly conflicts with something else that is also true.

In my business, for example, when my staff was at its largest, I had a group of four or five women employees. This circle of women was one of the great blessings of my business life because, despite being the boss, working with these women allowed me to collapse into what was most familiar. We were *not* like a well-oiled machine, but more like molecules of water flowing in a river. Every woman who has been in a strong women's circle knows how this feels. There was no competition and no overt hierarchy, just the ebb and flow of work as each in turn took on more weight when another was overloaded or feeling a little down and out.

In marked contrast to this circle was a male employee who was a brilliant radio and television production manager. He was a personal friend of my husband and business partner, Bob. Bob needed this man to handle production details while Bob stayed focused on the clients and developed the creative content of the commercials. This partnership worked extremely well—for them. For the women, this man was a perpetual source of aggravation. They perceived him as someone who would not pick up the phone even if everyone else was occupied, and who insisted on having his own private space; whereas the women couldn't stand being out of line of sight from each other. From his point of view, he was necessarily focused on his work and did not have time for these distractions. In truth, he handled more complex technical details with minimal error than anyone I have ever known.

This conflict came to a head when we moved to a new office. I opted to give the production manager an inner office with no window in fairness to the women. In the old office the women had been crammed together, and he had had his own space. He was horrified. Having an office with a window suddenly became very important to him; he was beside himself. The women were equally furious at his insistence that he be given what he wanted. They assumed that he was only concerned with status. I wasn't so sure. For some people, a windowless room is impossibly claustrophobic. Luckily I was reading Tom Peters at the time. Peters believes that a president should serve employees—the people who are doing the real work on the line (Peters 1987). This idea gave me the solution to my problem. I took the inner office for myself and gave everyone else a window.

Now I am not particularly a heroine for having taken the inner office. I simply did not care where my office was. But my production manager did. I could not identify with his view of the world, but it was part of our total office reality. Thus I looked for a way to accommodate both his "either-or" mind-set and the women's "both-and" mind-set. My diffuse awareness allowed me to make a decision that in the long run worked better for my people than a decision based on my idea of what was the right or wrong way to organize our office. There was always tension and an uneasy peace at best about the different ways that the women and this production manager viewed their working relationship, but I believe our office was alive and real. I could not bring myself to squash either his inner life or theirs by choosing all one way or the other.

DIFFUSE AWARENESS AS AN ASSET IN BUSINESS

What is the benefit of this diffuse awareness? It may give us a more complete picture of reality, but does it not leave us in a state of tension, even paralysis in business? Sometimes, yes, if we hold onto it too tightly and do not see the dynamic interplay between diffuse awareness and focused consciousness. For the company executive who observed his female managers as better at process and his male managers as better at leading the charge, each tendency had its place and its own importance in the work of his firm. In a crisis the men were better at letting go of established priorities and working all night to solve a problem or take advantage of a new opportunity. The women, on the other hand, were better at developing a process that was designed to work for the long term; while the men would be asking, "When can we have it?" before it was complete.

On some occasions taking action for the sake of doing something can be a more dangerous course than wallowing in confusion, because it can lead us to believe that we are on the right track when we may be missing the track altogether. Buying the right mutual funds, for example, won't count for much if the whole economy goes under because of our national debt. Collaboration between diffuse awareness and focused consciousness can lead us to deeper and more lasting solutions to our most troublesome problems when those problems involve dynamic processes that are fluid and hard to pin down or when major shifts of historical proportions take us beyond what we already know.

When I think about the possibilities of such a collaboration between diffuse awareness and focused consciousness, I am reminded of what I said earlier, that the masculine energy focuses well on generating a *new* reality, while the feminine energy sees more clearly all of what really exists now, including what is not going to go away. A senior female manager at a leading-edge software company understood the importance of the feminine outlook. Working in a complex global market, in which change came in the form of sudden ninety-degree turns, she knew that her company must be able to make major decisions quickly or it would be out of business, perhaps not immediately, but inevitably within a few years. She was trying to get everyone in her company to look everything in the environment squarely in the eye and tell themselves the whole truth about what they saw, especially that portion of reality that made them feel the most despair. She had a strong, deeply spiritual faith that if the leaders in her company would not let themselves off the hook on this difficult and disturbing task, they *would* be able to solve their problems. If she succeeds in *her* difficult task of getting them to do this, she will have much to tell us about how the feminine diffuse awareness can expand the data field, so that the masculine focused consciousness can do its best work of generating a new solution or new direction that will really work for the future and not be just a stop-gap measure.

This capacity to see what is not going to go away is not unlike insisting that the emperor is wearing no clothes. We are so busy trying to make our businesses and the world what we want them to be, that we tend to miss some very important data. This situation may explain why we feel so helpless in the face of homelessness, joblessness, and the environmentally damaging production of useless stuff. We are not seeing outside of, behind, below, beyond, and around our present conceptions of growth and success—even of excellence and quality control. A non-recyclable product, for example, is a pollutant to our environment, however ingenious or well made it may be.

Again, diffuse awareness takes what it sees at face value and does not edit. It does not make a distinction that x is in the domain of business, and *y* is *not* in the domain of business. Everything is interconnected. Maybe we are not really missing any data, as I suggested above, but simply lose our grasp on the data we have, or withhold it, because we have bought the notion that only certain data belongs in the business environment.

We have all experienced the business meeting in which people were impatient to get back to the *real* work. But what *is* the real work of business? And what does business *really* affect? And what *really* affects business? An unhealthy physical environment, for example, or major social disruption in a community, will negatively affect businesses. A small business that has operated for a long time in one place is acutely aware of the interdependence between itself and the community around it. Are the physical resources that a company uses uncontaminated to start with, and does the company contaminate the resources the community needs to use? Do the schools produce the skilled workers the company needs, and does the company contribute enough to the financial base to support good schools? Are workers physically and psychologically healthy, and does the work they do at the company make them more or less so? Do people in the community have enough money to buy the company's products, and does the company contribute to the buying power of the community? And so on.

But these questions are easier to ignore in businesses that have grown large and interface with a sphere much larger than their immediate communities or even their regional or national economies. The global impact of the destruction of the rain forest, for example, is only a conceptual reality to us in the Northern Hemisphere. So, too, is the social dislocation in some Third World countries. As with the spread of AIDS, or even cancer, we cannot understand the real meaning of these problems until someone we know is affected.

Long term, everything that is happening around the world can impact our lives and our businesses for better or for worse, and our capacity to damage the whole global system at this point far exceeds our capacity to do so at the beginning of this century.

It is time now to use all the data at our disposal to solve the problems of the world and not confine our thinking just to what we can conceptualize rationally.

The most creative part of my work in my garden began when I went beyond drawing maps and started trusting my instincts to move plants in the moment even though I could not give a reason why I did so. What I am hoping for for all of us is that, wherever we find ourselves in business, we will each engage in the task of seeing the whole picture of our business reality. We need to strengthen this mental muscle called diffuse awareness so we can see the complete relationship between our businesses and the context in which they operate—local, regional, and even global.

We know that diffuse awareness allows us to tune in to everything that touches the lives of our children as we raise them in our families. I am equally confident that diffuse awareness will allow us to tune in to everything that touches the life of the whole earth system as we operate our businesses. I want us to think seriously about the possibility that this capacity for diffuse awareness could make the whole economic system much more responsive to the complex problems of the world. I believe that if we can make ourselves continue the difficult task of perceiving and acknowledging *everything* that is happening, however disturbing, we *will* be able to solve our problems.

Diffuse awareness, then, is an extraordinary potential tool. A way of perceiving reality as a field rather than as a series of points, diffuse awareness takes in the relationships *among* things as a central piece of information. This type of perception is at the heart of the feminine principle, but it is not the feminine principle in its entirety. Underneath diffuse awareness is a powerful feminine *value* that helps us understand what this diffuse awareness tool is designed to serve. This feminine value—the second ingredient of the feminine principle and the subject of the next chapter—is the feminine affirmation of life.

Chapter 3

The Quick of the Moment

Feminine wisdom is a continual affirmation of life, through its eternal readiness to respond to the quick of the moment; it is not communicated by the word or rite, but through presence and being.

—ROBERT STEIN, *Incest and Human Love*

The organizing principle behind diffuse awareness, and the real gift of the feminine, I think, is its loyalty not to ideas, but to life itself. In his videotape *On Men and Women*, with Marion Woodman, Robert Bly says, "When I look in the eyes of a woman, I see something profoundly fair. I am stunned at the decency women have in their attempt to be fair to their children, to the world. I am very moved by that" (Bly and Woodman 1992). I, in turn, was moved by his affirmation of the concern for the whole of life that I know I carry in my very bones and see in women everywhere.

In this chapter I look more closely at what it means to continually "affirm life," to be ready "to respond to the quick of the moment," and to communicate through "presence and being." Then I look at the ambivalence our culture feels about these attributes, and, finally, I consider how they can contribute value to the workplace.

Feminine affirmation of life, the ability to respond to the quick of the moment, and communication through presence and being are superbly summed up for me in an image I have of a student in a high school American history class that I taught on the depression. This beautiful child-woman was barely five feet tall, with bright blue-green eyes, a creamy complexion, and a wild head of curly red hair. As the class discussed how the farmers were dumping milk to protest that they were not getting paid enough to live on, this young woman looked up incredulously and said, "Why didn't they just give the milk to the people who were starving in the cities in exchange for the things that they needed?" Another student chimed in, "But Tracy, that would be Communism!"

Not bound by history or collective principles, the feminine sees newly what is needed to support life in the *particular* situation, here and now, and it responds accordingly. Then, the abstracting, generating masculine, so the theory goes, can conceptualize that response and give it form. The partnership is perfect, but too often we bypass the feminine action of spontaneous response and move directly to the collective principles we have already agreed upon, as the above comment about Communism so richly illustrates. In business we are actually embarrassed when there is an outburst (and it usually is an outburst) like Tracy's. We label it cute, but naive, and dismiss it. Remember if you will, the first (and probably the last) time you had such a response to a situation in business and your outburst was met by awkward silence, condescending smiles, or outright laughter.

Yet we also all know that there are immeasurable rewards—in our private lives certainly—for the kinds of presence to the here and now that allow us just to "be" and to respond to life spontaneously, to the quick of the moment. For me, this reward is never so apparent as when I am driving through Vermont in early October. Leaving my home in Tunbridge to bring a computer to Rochester for repair, I drive westward over the peak of a ridge. When I reach the top and start down the other side, an expanse of the Green Mountains opens up in front of me. To either side of me are maple, birch, and beech trees, showing the brilliant oranges, reds, and yellows of the fall. Far in the distance, the mountains, illuminated by morning light, are a muted orange gradually becoming more blue as they roll away and merge with the sky. I can feel spirit quicken within me as I pass over the peak, and my body almost seems to rise with the exhilaration of the scene as I continue my descent. It never fails to happen, no matter what the season, so long as I am not so deeply lost in thought that I fail to see the view at all. I often drive over this peak with songs from the brothers at the Benedictine Priory in Weston, Vermont, playing at full volume, or listening to Paul Winter's music from *Missa Gaia*, especially the song "The Blue Green Hills of Earth."

When I am truly present to the view in front of me, I experience this view bodily and soulfully. In fact, I cannot distinguish between body and soul. An important aspect of presence and being is the capacity to *experience* reality as a whole. The central sensation is one of aliveness, of deep appreciation, of affirmation, of wanting to respond. In this state it never occurs to me that physical reality is less important than spiritual reality, no matter how much we may conceptualize spirituality as transcending the physical and therefore being more important. To me, reality on "both sides"—within life and beyond it, as the ancient Celts perceived it—is filled with profound mystery.

It is easy to find examples of how women and men experience this sense of mystery outside of business, but what plunges people into a similar ecstatic experience at work? I sometimes envy those computer techies who seem to experience their programming activities as divine encounters. I can see this among scientists and mathematicians, too, as well as artists, but I rarely see such bliss in normal business situations.

From my early school days, I have found the compartmentalization of private life and public life—the separation of spirituality and feeling from the classroom or office—difficult to deal with. Sometime before ten years of age, I sat in my bedroom looking out the window and wondered, Why am I here? I wasn't asking why was I in this house or with this family or in this country. I had in my mind a sense of a much larger reality than the earth or even the physical realm of the universe, and I was genuinely perplexed about the question, as children are before they discount such questions as foolish. Why did I end up on earth? for what purpose? I have never been able to believe that my purpose is simply to save my soul or fulfill my karma. I want to know why there is such a thing as physical reality. What purpose does *that* serve in the larger scheme of things? It matters to me how things turn out here on earth. I want to give it my full attention, my love, and my capacity to work.

This feeling of immediate connection to, and intense involvement with, the environment is the feminine affirmation of life. Robert Stein is right that this aspect of the feminine is not communicated well by words. It is something that is *felt* and that is most truly expressed, or communicated, by us when we are simply being present to, that is, fully aware of, the mystery of life—in the external environment of earth and sky and within our bodies. Since it is not possible to be aware of this mystery of life without experiencing our own being as a part of that mystery, presence itself contributes to conscious being. Thus when people in our midst are genuinely present to the mystery around them, their being radiates outward and communicates their authenticity to us. It is not surprising, then, that we so often seek out gurus. It is their presence and being, not their ideas, that we hope will communicate itself to us.

Experiencing presence and being is too essential an aspect of living not to have an application to business. In fact, I think it is essential to business, and I want to ask the same questions of my business that I ask of my life in general. Why am I in this business? What purpose does it serve in the larger scheme of things? How can my capacity to work contribute to the well-being of the whole?

IMPACT OF THE SPIRIT/MATTER SPLIT

Experiencing physical and spiritual reality as an integrated whole is not the norm, certainly not in our Western culture, and if I tell the truth, I myself don't experience this reality most of the time. I seem conditioned not to feel quite at home here on earth. It is as if I have one foot here and one foot some other place to which I feel linked by my consciousness. I hear people repeatedly insist that we are not animals, or that we are not "just" animals, as if to identify at all with nature is to get stuck in it and to lose our claim to a spiritual base. Like so many others I know, I feel driven to distinguish myself from the rest of animal life and the whole earth system within which I live. Yet the more diminished physical matter is for us, the more addicted we are to things, perhaps to make up for our lack of connection with life. Viewing the physical world as dead, and on some level beneath us, contributes to our willingness to use our natural resources for so many consumer goods (Lonergan 1987). And as we create more and more advanced material lifestyles as barriers between ourselves and nature, we simultaneously deplete the physical resources we depend on to live.

In this uneasy climate, the feminine capacity for presence and being, here and now, and the obvious fact that women give birth through their bodies have long resulted in a negative association between the feminine and the physical world. We seem to believe that loyalty to one or the other—spirit or matter—is a choice that we have to make, and it is pretty obvious which we believe is the superior choice. Starting with Eve and working up through the witch hunts into the present, woman has been seen as the symbol of an evil, corrupting quality of nature. We have made a lot of progress, but there still remains a profound ambivalence about the feminine. This ambivalence, I believe, tells us more about our troubled relationship with nature, with being here now in this world, than it does about man's attitude toward woman. This is not an easy idea to grasp. Because of the negative association, the wounds of women have been so great that we have a hard time separating what has to do with women and what has to do with the psyche and the cultural history of the "other." Some of the leading male scholars in the Men's movement have refined this further by showing that our Western culture values only the mental and spiritual masculine traits as characterized by Apollo and has cut men off from their chthonic, or earth-based, masculinity as characterized by Dionysus and others (Monick 1987).

Though I have never been able to identify with this split wholeheartedly, it has deeply influenced me. Whether male or female, each of us tends to experience feminine presence and being as a great pool of physical and emotional chaos that we would like to avoid. It takes us away from what we consider our real business: developing focused consciousness. Such feelings call to my mind all those horrible quicksand movies of my childhood, which made me vividly imagine creepy things in the muck that would bite at my feet and body as I went under.

There is a constant tension in me, then, between what I perceive as moving onward and upward through consciousness and being dragged back down into some primordial past. This reminds me of a dream in which I was hit from behind in an automobile accident, hurt my legs, and subsequently found that my whole abdomen was jammed up, just as I had experienced in real life not long before in a fender bender. In my work life I often feel as if I have been hit from behind *psychically*—by education and the culture generally—such that my body is jammed up, in a tense position anticipating having to perform perfectly. This obsession with perfection—this striving for the perfect performance—propels my mind perpetually away from awareness of the here and now and toward mental images of the future, as I would like that future to be. Constant engagement in mentally constructing the future separates me from spontaneous relationships with people, and from the healing and forgiving earth that stretches out in front of me here in Vermont and invites me daily to walk like other animals upon its surface and delight in its inspirations.

I can see this drivenness everywhere. Although it is most apparent in a few extreme colleagues and clients, if I tell myself the truth, I know this drivenness has inhabited me to some degree from my earliest school days to my current business life. This is the *normal* condition of business. No wonder there are so many stress-related diseases.

FEMININE PASSION

We often think that this drivenness is a result of greed, but its roots, I believe, are much more deeply imbedded in our split view of reality—of spirit and matter as separated and alienated from each other. If I am right, curing this drivenness will involve learning to feel more at home here on the earth and accepting our place in nature, in much the same way that people who are involved with the Twelve Step program accept a higher power. This task of reconciling spirit and matter is hardly the exclusive domain of the feminine, but the feminine affirmation of life can help us with this problem because it instinctively recognizes that a spiritual essence or mystery permeates matter.

Human sexuality offers us a metaphorical example of how inseparable spirit and matter are in feminine consciousness. In a presentation at a seminar program at the Harvard Divinity School, Margaret Miles showed that St. Augustine's *Confessions*, one of the cornerstones of Western spirituality, is full of male erotic imagery (Miles 1990). She so intrigued me with this idea that I read the *Confessions* myself, and I could see that St. Augustine's early sensual experience provided the images—of hunger, passion, and ecstasy—through which he was able to describe the development of his spirituality. Ironically, he redirected his erotic energy upward toward God, and, ultimately, forsook sensuality without seeming to be conscious that his sensual experience was the root of much of his spiritual imagery.

Miles then challenged her listeners to consider these questions: What is the nature of *female* desire? and What form would spirituality based on female desire take? In Western spirituality, based on St. Augustine's model, we have linked matter/body, and erotic feelings that come with the body, with debasement and fall from grace, and we have redirected energy upward, away from matter. But this image is problematic for females, whose sexual energy is not directed outward from the body like a man's.

In two ancient customs we can see how spirituality was handled differently for each gender. Some early male spiritual initiations took the form of real or symbolic castration. The idea was for the masculine energy to give itself over to the Goddess, that is, to give up its power to seize what it wanted, in order to be in service to, and in communion with, the divine feminine principle. By contrast, female spiritual initiations sometimes took the form of temple or sacred prostitution. Before she could marry, a woman would go to the temple, where any man could select her as his spiritual-sexual partner. The idea was for the feminine energy to give up possessiveness and, as a human representative of the Goddess, give freely of itself to any man in a sacred encounter.

The man, then, needed to learn restraint. The woman needed to learn to be an instrument of archetypal love and not use her feminine powers purely to possess or hold a man. The two orientations are fundamentally different. The masculine gives up bodily power and, like St. Augustine, redirects its energy toward the divine. The feminine immerses itself in matter and lets divine energy flow through human form.

What does it mean to immerse ourselves in matter and let divine energy flow through our human form? In her lecture, Miles said that St. Augustine's "formulation of the spiritual life as a withdrawal from attachment to the world has played a role in creating the present condition of the earth, a planet in ecological and nuclear crisis" (Miles 1990, 9). What she believes we need today is a spiritual model "emphasizing attention to, and affection for, the vulnerable and threatened earth, by energizing committed labor for peace and justice, and by illuminating the spiritual discipline of loving relationship and community"

(Miles 1990, 9). This is the spiritual model of letting divine energy flow through human form—onto the earth instead of away from of it.

Holding this image in our minds—the image of immersing ourselves in matter and letting divine energy flow through our human form—can help us to understand the power of the feminine affirmation of life to transcend the mental boundaries between spirit and matter. A conceptual understanding of the global environmental crisis, however important, will not be enough. Our concepts need to be grounded in an *experience* of the physical and spiritual realms as an interconnected whole.

ATTACHMENT TO LIFE AS A BUSINESS VALUE

Another way of thinking about this feminine immersion in matter, the experience of physical and spiritual life as an interconnected whole, is as attachment to life. I like to use this phrase because my mind immediately jumps to the word "detachment," the apparent opposite of "attachment." Detachment is the key goal of not only St. Augustine's spiritual model but of many other spiritual systems as well. It has always seemed to me that detachment does not have much meaning if we were never attached to something in the first place.

The profound attachment that the feminine feels for life, here and now, comes with us into the secular world of business whether we want it to or not. Attachment to life is more than ambition or ethics or good service. It has always mattered to me that my employees, my clients, and my vendors do well for deeper reasons than profit or my reputation for good performance. It matters just because it matters. This concern goes beyond conventional ethics to what Carol Gilligan describes as the feminine "activity of care." Women, she says, are constantly looking to see to whom or what they have been *unresponsive*, rather than gauging whether or not they have been fair. The fairness that Gilligan's colleague, Lawrence Kohlberg, found as a central theme in moral development among men is not the same as the fairness that Bly saw in women. What Bly observed as women's fairness is what Gilligan observes as women's immersion in a web of relationship in which they want everyone's needs to be met (Gilligan 1993). My desire to find a way to meet the needs of both my female administrative staff and my male production manager is a good example.

Fairness in the public world of men means that everyone has a fair chance, but there is no guarantee of being cared for if you fail. Men in mainstream business have found ways to compensate for this—through friendship and enormous generosity—when their colleagues periodically fall through the cracks in our current system, but the deep desire to change this whole situation is largely in the domain of the feminine.

The implications of this feminine desire to have everyone's needs met go beyond personal care in the family or even personal care for individuals in the workplace. The care of the whole planetary system stands to benefit. If we added the feminine sense of fairness to the masculine sense of fairness in a dynamic mix in our public life, what would we have? For example, what opportunities, other than institutional welfare, would we create for the inevitable losers in a basically fair economic game? Furthermore, what proactive steps would we take—not just in the form of government regulations—to ensure that harmful products were not introduced to our environment, or that the earth's resources will not be depleted? If we truly experienced the earth's resources in the same way that we experience our children, what would we do to protect them?

I want to be challenged by the very real and exciting competition of the masculine world, but I also want to be known and valued as a creature of the earth regardless of what I produce. When I unexpectedly come across an animal in the woods, I am struck dumb by the wonder of it. I pick up every detail of the shape and texture of the animal. It is a sacred encounter; I do *not* stop to assess its personality flaws or its potential failure of nerve or lack of ambition. In public life a conscious feminine attitude, which continually affirms life and can respond to the quick of the moment, is capable of experiencing the whole earth and each human animal in this way too. We experience our children in this way every day, even though their failings and traumas cause us pain and anxiety. Why not our employees and colleagues, our vendors and our clients?

I have a theory that this capacity to continually affirm life reveals itself in a special way when we look at what we *want*. In fact, I would say that wanting what we want—regardless of how naive or utopian it might seem—is part of the job of the feminine. I used to feel discomfort about the fact that women can usually get what they want from men. It seemed manipulative. But it may be that there is something deeper in the design. The feminine seems to know instinctually what is needed for life, particularly in those cases—such as Tracy's response to the shortage of goods in the depression—where our concepts and principles are not adequate to deal with a new situation. Maybe the most effective way to get the masculine energy—both within us and without—to create what is needed is just to want it, and not hide that we want it. We *do* need to be careful in evaluating what we want, to look deeply and not superficially, but not necessarily abdicate on the wanting.

Wanting what we want, we might assume, is easy, but if we look at our lives closely, we might be surprised at how difficult it really is, especially for women. Gilligan's study of women's moral development sheds some important light on why this is so. There are three stages of female moral development, she explains. The first two stages we know well: the first is girlish selfishness, and the second is the self*less*ness women are taught as they grow up. This second stage of selflessness, the "activity of care," tends, in practical reality, to mean putting oneself last and paying attention to everyone else's needs first. The third stage requires a paradoxical shift from the second stage; this stage is a stumbling block for many women, because it involves including *oneself* in the "everyone" who has a right to have basic needs met (Gilligan 1993).

Women are very good at giving lip service to the idea that their needs are as important as everyone else's, without really living it. Men have told me that they are mystified and sometimes driven crazy by some women's inability to say what they want in the business arena. If you are female, consider the last time you engaged in a real estate negotiation, for example, or any other kind of negotiation for that matter. I caught myself in such a situation recently. When being cross-examined by a friend about the potential sale of my house, I found the following questions in my mind: How disappointed will my realtor be, after all his work marketing my house, if I don't accept the offer for my house that he has presented? What will it mean for the potential buyers, particularly for their timetable, if they have to start over looking for another house to buy? And if I *do* accept the offer, what will it mean for my tenant? I am not suggesting that these are inappropriate questions to be asking. But my friend pointed out to me that I was not considering my own needs in the same light. Many women, Gilligan rightly points out, have a difficult time contributing to someone else's difficulty or inconvenience. Getting to Gilligan's third stage of moral development means accepting oneself as a creature on the earth who has a right to take up space. Taking up space inevitably means having an impact on the lives of others, both good and bad, because sooner or later there will be a conflict between what I want and what someone else wants. It is the negative impact on others that women try to avoid.

If we don't say what we want, we think we can avoid having a negative impact. Unfortunately that means we won't have much of a positive impact either. It is important to ask ourselves what positive impact we might have if we started saying what we really want in the workplace; because when what we want is not purely selfish, the wanting itself may serve life. And business is part of life, not separate from it.

What I want in business is a real sense of community, of knowing and being known to my fellow workers, vendors, and clients. I ache for this. I also want simple natural beauty—inside and outside of my office—so I can feel really alive and connected to the world in which I work. Having useful work is critical to me; I want to know that what I am doing contributes to life in some way. I want time for myself, to reflect, which means that I need a much slower pace than is normal for most businesses. Finally, I have two desires that will be the hardest to produce: economic justice and a future for our children. I would give up a lot if I knew it meant that others would really have more of their basic needs met, both now and in the future. What would you add to the list?

Feminine "affirmation of life," the readiness to respond to "the quick of the moment," and communication through "presence and being" are three images that point us toward a deeper understanding of the core feminine attachment to life itself, an attachment that is counter to our mental tendency to separate spirit and matter as if they were in opposition to each other. Through these three images, I have tried, as if reenacting the *Magic Eye* exercise, to provide a more three-dimensional sense of this feminine quality of attachment in which the physical and spiritual worlds are experienced and appreciated as one integrated whole. Experiencing the world in this way sets us up for an exquisite and active, not a passive, receptivity to life. It is this receptivity—the ability to accept and even honor the cycles of life—that is the subject of our next chapter.

Chapter 4

Accepting the Cycles of Life

Life is difficult. . . . Once we truly know that life if difficult—
once we truly understand and accept it—then life is no longer
difficult. Because once it is accepted, the fact that life is difficult
no longer matters.

—SCOTT PECK, *The Road Less Traveled*

I once worked with a consultant who had a real gift for getting
my partner and me to look at our current mind-set and "break
through" to something new. At one point I was observing a
dramatic negative turn in my business, and I joked with him that
after giving me a chance to experience a great deal of success, the
universe now seemed to be saying, "Now you are ready to see if
you can deal with disaster!" The consultant challenged me by
asking, "Can you design a business for success without the cycle
of failure?"

I intuitively felt he had asked the wrong question. Maybe
you *can* design a business for success without the cycle of failure,
though I doubt it, but would you want to? What information
might you miss in the process?

Seeking mental breakthrough and applying our will to implement the resulting strategy is, to me, the best aspect of the masculine energy. It pulls us toward new understanding; it gives meaning and sets up creative action. At a business group's community-building workshop in the early 1990s, however, I learned that building real community can help solve situations that fall outside the influence of active will, and real community can be generated only through patience. If proper attention is paid to creating the right atmosphere, the important thing can happen on its own. This is the part of life that is mysterious to us, which controls and guides *us* rather than the other way around. This is the part of life that the feminine holds in loving and patient hands.

Sometimes the most difficult thing about life is simply accepting it, particularly its cyclical nature. In this chapter I look at the turbulent nature of that part of life that is outside our active will, and I use four metaphors, starting with the feminine metaphor of birthing. The second metaphor is death and dying, the hardest of the cycles to accept. The third metaphor is built on the story of a girls athletic program that has led me personally to a greater understanding of what it might feel like to stay engaged in life while we are buffeted about by cycles we do not yet understand. And the last metaphor is darkness as a womb image, which we can use to help sustain our courage. Throughout I will talk about the implications for business of these images and metaphors from the feminine domain and how we might consciously hold them in the workplace.

GIVING BIRTH

I have never had children of my own, and my two sisters who have children adopted them. So my direct experience with birthing was nonexistent until a friend invited me and my husband to be present when she gave birth to her one and only child. That birth took three days. I was proud of myself for not getting squeamish, but I *was* sobered. My office kept calling me to find out the results, and they groaned each time I reported that the baby still had not been born. When I stayed overnight with my sister, who lived near the hospital, I told her that she had definitely made the right choice in adopting her two children—in my view!

I have heard enough stories to know that the birth experience varies enormously from woman to woman. One friend barely got to the hospital before her first child, and all subsequent children, were born. Another, a nurse, had enough presence of mind to order the anesthesiologist out of the delivery room because she knew she was too far along to benefit from his expensive services. Other women have had to deal with cesareans after long and hard labor. Many women throughout the ages have died giving birth; while others have gone uncomplainingly back to the fields within days or even hours of delivering.

A nurse told me about a common pattern when women hit what is known as "transition," one of the last stages of labor. They have this unrelenting urge to get up and leave the hospital, to say, "That's it. I quit. I'm not doing this anymore." As humorous as that sounds, it is a real phenomenon, as many women know.

There *is* a certain humor to all this along with the pain, and a wonderful overarching knowledge that the birthing process will come to an end eventually. There is also the strong probability, though no guarantee, that the result will be a healthy child, who will bring instant joy, and that the mother will survive the ordeal.

This perspective is less clear in other creative struggles in life, but the cycle of pain, uncertainty, and ultimate joy is probably no less true in all our creative endeavors. Take change in our business organizations, for instance. Despite some new buzz words—"excellence," "quality control," "empowerment"—we are still trying to bypass a real birthing process in this arena. We prefer a birth like that of the Greek goddess Athena, who was born out of the head of Zeus. The head we are comfortable with. Thus we embrace innovations with the hope that they will be successful techniques to painlessly enable employees to produce more—better, faster, and cheaper. A birthing process that is messy and uncertain, and that would give us a whole new system that would eventually have a life of its own, beyond us, like the child's life outside it's mother's body, is not what we have in mind.

Yet the birth process inspires awe in us precisely because we do not control the end product. And time and time again, nature proves to us that it can do better than we can. Using our best planning abilities we could not envision the unique mix of characteristics that so often emerges from the womb in an individual human being.

Nature produces human beings according to its own design, and the same may be true for economic systems, although we do have more opportunity here to interfere and thwart the intention of nature—but only for so long. Economics, after all, involves the distribution of goods and services. If an economic system cannot effectively manage the flow of necessities to almost everyone and solve our essential physical problems, it cannot last, even if it has lasted for hundreds of years already. "Everyone" used to mean one's tribe; most recently it has meant one's country. But more and more, "everyone" means all the people on the whole planet, since so many countries are now linked together in so many ways. As our global consciousness is strengthened, we can see that our current use and distribution systems are severely strained. They serve the Northern and Western Hemispheres far more effectively than they do the Eastern and Southern Hemispheres, and they have not kept pace with solving the environmental problems that these very same systems have created.

Nature, through the human species, will have to give birth to a different economic reality before the planet self-destructs. Is it any wonder that we are experiencing labor pains? Our "transition" seems so hard to some of us that we can see no way out but to quit—if only we could! Others are not yet even aware that we are collectively pregnant.

DEATH AND DYING

As we move into the future, I am remembering the four maxims that my husband and I worked out after we experienced that three-day birth.

1. *Life is difficult.* This is the very first line of Scott Peck's *The Road Less Traveled* (Peck 1985), and the best. I have had it pasted on my wall for years.
2. *Go with the flow.* The most you can control are your own responses. The process has a life of its own, and it will keep going whether you quit or not.
3. *Rest during the onslaughts.* It takes energy to manage the pain and effort, so conserve your energy.
4. *Don't lust after desired outcomes.* From an ancient Celtic rune, this is good advice in almost any circumstance, but never more than during labor. It will happen when it happens.

Trying to follow my own advice, I struggle with these things in my business. I have to admit that this feels more like dying to me than birthing because I cannot see far enough ahead to know what new life I may be carrying. When a large client backed out of a contract because of changes in its own economic environment, leaving my company with a huge unsold inventory, with almost no time to resell it, I became willful. I *will* sell this inventory quickly, I said to myself, and I *will* enforce this contract. I know this feeling well. I watched as one customer after another said no to our proposals, and I saw the list of possibilities dwindle. It was as if I could feel a tight wire across my chest that I could not push through, but I could not stop trying. I had to fight this. I looked into the future and saw no other options except humiliation and bankruptcy, and I examined my whole life and cataloged all the things that I had ever done wrong. For surely this was my fault, and it was my responsibility to make it right.

I will probably be struggling with this challenge my whole life—trying to experience an economic setback as the same thing as any other unexpected turn in life, not as a personal failure of my character. Dying, real or symbolic, seems to come before new birth as winter comes before spring. Elisabeth Kubler-Ross, and others who work with the terminally ill, say that there are several stages one goes through in accepting death: denial, anger, bargaining, depression and acceptance (Kubler-Ross 1991). I look around at American business and see so many of us somewhere in the first three stages, mostly in the first. Somewhat smugly we watched the Russians go through the collapse of a system that would not work for their future. But underneath I felt uneasy, and I know others did too, because our system may not work for the future either, certainly not for the future sustainability of the planet. We simply are using up too many of our physical resources too fast to continue following our current path for much longer.

In coming to terms with my situation, I asked myself, Did I fail to use good business judgment? Or, Is the business I am operating no longer viable or useful for the future? If the latter is true, can I grieve it so I can let it go instead of hanging on and trying to make it work so I can avoid the disruption of major change? Can I tell the truth to the bank about my balance sheet and take my chances that they will continue to have enough confidence in me to support my business financially? Can I let go of my house and my other possessions, even my garden, until I can recover and find a new path that *is* viable? Can I let go of the particular opinion I want others to have of me as a successful businesswoman? Shouldn't I, after all, be someone with ever increasing capital, contacts, and resources—someone who has amusing dinner-hour stories to tell about being confronted by tough situations, but who has never really had to consider that the bottom could totally fall out?

These are important considerations because it takes time to replace what is no longer functional—maybe even decades, not just years. Trusting the universe in this context means something deeper than expecting a happy coincidence to occur next week. It is very difficult to hold the images of birthing and dying in my mind when I am engaged in my business life. I am far too entrenched in the culture's view of continuous progress, and especially of its view of how much money I should have in my fifties, to take to this kind of dying and birthing easily.

But learning to hold onto and work with these images in our work life is important. The difficulty in seeing and accepting the whole picture of reality, including its cycles, is not unique to any of us. It exists throughout the larger business environment. I have belonged to business organizations devoted to global sustainability that have held weekend meetings in the most expensive hotels in America, whose members were served food transported from across the country, if not the world, at great energy costs. Now these people are not hypocrites; they simply do not see the incongruity. The same is true for high-level executives who sincerely suffer over massive layoffs yet cannot see any way to alter the commonly accepted, but very expensive business culture in which we all swim, a business culture that could eventually sink us. Does it make sense, for example, that some executives end up getting salary increases and bonuses after downsizing their workforces following a merger?

RANDOLPH GIRLS BASKETBALL: LEARNING ON THE COURT

I have found—in an unexpected place—a very helpful metaphor for simultaneously staying in the action while flowing with the cycles of life when we don't understand where they begin and where they will end. The Randolph Union High School in Vermont has a girls basketball team that plays better than my husband Bob, by his own account, played on his best day. This is not a dainty half-court version of basketball, but the real thing—

superb ballhandling, precision passes, and three-point baskets "from another zip code," as one enthusiastic reporter described it. I am impressed. In fact, I am a rabid fan. You would have to understand just how obtuse I am about sports in general to get the irony of my passion. Larry Bird and Big Bird, it's all the same to me.

But I love these girls. I love them for what they are learning that I am trying so hard to learn myself—how to move my body and mind with mastery and in coordination with others for the good of the whole. What a sweet sight they are as they move down the court, pass the ball around, switch positions, and move in for the shot. The skill of their hands makes holding and passing that ball look so easy. In midair, amidst players intent on defending against them, they pull down the rebounds swift and sure. They know how to dribble and step in just the right sequence and number of steps the rules allow. There is precision yet lightness, perpetual movement yet fierce groundedness to this game when it is played well.

The girls are also learning how to surrender to the coaching that will allow them to know what they are capable of. What an amazing thing. I watch the coach yell harsh commands to them from the sideline, and I try to imagine what it would be like to suspend my own thought process and do with my body what someone else instructs me to do, and then feel in my nerves and muscles a new set of movements I had not experienced before. I am fascinated by this. I want to learn what it takes for these young women to stay focused on their *own* game despite everything else that goes on around them. I find myself identifying with them totally, even as I am also an observer.

When I muse on these things, I have in mind, of course, a bigger game than basketball. I have in mind, too, a bigger game than career success and personal financial security, a bigger game even than a strong GNP in a global marketplace. For me the truly big game is planetary survival and evolution. It is not lost on me that survival itself may not be possible if we fail to take the next evolutionary step. A great defense, though vital, is rarely all that is needed to win.

In many ways I hate this metaphor in which winning and losing is so central. But since reality is the scorekeeper in the game I want to play, I have to acknowledge that some of the human species' failures to grow *may* indeed be fatal. I don't like it, but there it is. I would strongly prefer that the human species not have to become extinct in order for life to flourish.

What, then, might stop us from our own evolution? Para-doxically, it may be that we will be done in by our inability to go beyond our win/lose obsession—our inability, that is, to surren-der to the cycles of failure that cleanse us of our errors in perceiv-ing reality. These cycles also clear out those perceptions that were valid once but are now outdated. Could we lose everything in the long run because we are so sure that winning, for the individual and the group, is everything?

Looking at my own life, I ask, What does winning mean in the foggy assumptions that rule my day-to-day existence? A nice house, a certain amount of money in the bank, future business on the horizon. But if I keep the metaphor of the Randolph girls in my mind, I can see that a season in which I play only games that I know I can win will not be the best kind of season for learning how to go beyond what I already know. What in the future will I sacrifice, perhaps unwittingly, because I am obsessed with winning every single game today? In business, winning every single game means never having to risk that nice house, a com-fortable amount of money in the bank, and future business that I can count on. On the personal level, I may lose work that I love; a basketball player will never know, for example, if she has a great layup shot if she never tries it. On a larger level, if I, along with everyone else, continue to hang onto the lifestyle levels that are the current measure of success, the loss could be depletion of resources and unalterable damage to our planetary systems.

Another big obstacle to our evolution could be our certainty about the value of personal independence as we see it in western culture. In our economic life we see two basic options, one championed by free enterprise and capitalism, and one by the government-controlled economies of communism and socialism. In our mutually exclusive worldviews we count on individual self-reliance, on the one hand, or we depend on the state to control class myopia and greed, on the other.

But it may be that both worldviews are becoming irrelevant. Neither system, for example, is as sophisticated about channeling human potential as is the game of basketball, where interdependence is not just something nice or charitable or ethical but the very definition of how things get done. On the court a star player multiplies her impact when she lets others set up her shot or even when she passes off to other less skilled players who are in a better position to shoot. The setup takes cooperation and coordination; it is also a beautiful thing to watch.

For a long time, in business I was sensitive about my autonomy. I felt I should learn to do everything in order to prove my worth as a business player. Now, well over a decade later, I appreciate more and more what my partner does much better than I can. In particular, my lack of skill as a salesperson has far more to do with my introversion than with the fact that I'm female, but it certainly did not look that way to me at the start. Even so, there have been a few occasions when I was the logical person to handle a sale, because I was, figuratively speaking, closer to the basket, perhaps because of the particular personality of the buyer or some other factor. And there are times when my partner can see more clearly in the financial domain, probably precisely because he is not immersed in it all the time. Over time, we have become both more autonomous in our functions in the company and respectful of each other's strengths and more willing to take in the feedback and insights of the other.

The shift to interdependence is occurring everywhere throughout our political and economic systems. Self-reliance is no longer enough to produce a vital, life-enhancing business that will make it into the next century. Not even nations are wholly independent anymore, let alone individual businesses. But we do not yet have the consciousness to see what this means fully, and thus we cannot take full advantage of our growing interdependence both within and outside our businesses.

What we need—and what I believe we are moving toward—is a whole new frame for our economic life. Just as 1990's girls basketball is a far cry from 1960's half-court version, I believe the economic frame for the future will be as different from our capitalist model as our industrial model was different from the old manor systems of Europe.

But we won't get into this new economic model without surrendering to a certain amount of dying and birthing. Women are good at this. They have been birthing and tending to the dying for centuries. Also, what women have long viewed as a liability—the persistent cultural view that women do not really have to succeed in business in order to succeed in life—may actually be an asset here, because most women have less position at stake in the current economic structure. Having less position at stake usually results in less visibility and not being listened to by those in positional power, but it also allows for more personal flexibility. As times change, and crises appear that cannot be solved by known strategies, those in positional power may become more open to feminine views and experiences; thus women may be able to help men break out of a game plan into which we are all locked by tradition. Or women, and likeminded men, may break out of traditional structures altogether and form their own experiments, not unlike the totally unexpected revolutions in Eastern Europe. Who would have believed just a decade ago that communist regimes could be overthrown with so little bloodshed?

What we all need to do, in my view, is learn to let the forces of life coach us to a new understanding of what complex systems we are capable of. In the metaphor of basketball, this means being willing to lose some games on the way to the finals, maybe even being willing to risk what we now define as too basic to lose: our businesses, our homes, our livelihoods and lifestyles, even our worldviews and personal sense of identity.

The risk, of course, is that if we put these things on the line—and if we lose too many regular season games—we won't make it to the finals at all; but the larger truth is that there is risk either way. If we want to give birth to something new, we have to get pregnant first, and every pregnancy carries with it the danger of miscarriage.

The finals for the human species will likely take place after we are gone, and only our children and grandchildren will know for sure if our strategies for winning today actually work in the long run. For my part, I am trying to put my faith in the model of the young women who are opening themselves up daily to new learning on the court.

LOVING THE DARK AS COMFORT FOR MY SOUL

Living with birthing and dying is not easy. What can help us stay the course is using diffuse awareness and presence and being to perceive, and then hold in our minds, the largest images we can find for the totality of life. A high-level manager of a major corporation said the following of his female business partner when they started a business of their own:

> She has an absolute faith in God, Spirit, the Universe, however you want to describe it. This is the underlying foundation that allows her to be such an optimist, and maintain her playfulness and humor. Underneath the effervescence is a powerfully focused will directed toward spiritual growth. She integrates it with her business and her life. The level of integration has been both a challenge and an inspiration to me.

Most of us carry some image of this overarching integration that can help us ward off despair. What comes to my mind is the vast darkness of space, the very womb of existence. I have always thought that the dark has gotten a bad rap in mythology and spirituality. I have put down more than one book that was so preoccupied with images of light and so hostile to images of darkness that I could not continue. Darkness is where germination takes place.

In the late 1980s, when I owned a cottage on an island off the coast of Massachusetts where there was no electricity and therefore no ambient light, I fell in love with the dark. I would spend hours at night standing on my front porch listening to the sound of the ocean and peering out into my yard where the trees cast shadowy shapes on the land. I seemed to be more conscious of the three dimensionality of the landscape at night than in the daytime. I leaned backward over the railing of the porch and looked upward past the roofline and the stars into infinity. Now I do the same thing in rural Vermont, accompanied by the sound of the brooks, which is deafening in the night but only a background noise by day. I look not only at the sky but at the outline of the hills, and I contemplate their substance and how they came into being. There is an essence to things—some people have called it interiority—that I am more aware of in the dark than in the light.

On the island, there was a passageway to my house through a grove of large trees. At night, as I walked through, I felt like I was in a birth canal. Where I now live in Vermont, there is a winding half-mile of tree-lined dirt road to my neighbors, an ascending slope to one side and a sharp descent to the brook on the other. We walk this road at night without a flashlight for the sheer joy of being so deliciously enclosed, sometimes by stillness, sometimes by howling winds in a blizzard. Either way, my body can sense the vibrant energy of the fir trees on either side. These trees are never more alive to me than when I am walking through them in the dark.

And the winter solstice is my most sacred time of the year— that longest night of the year in late December, when the sun is farthest away from the Northern Hemisphere. To the ancients, for whom the earth was the center of the universe, the night of the solstice was the point at which the sun stopped its journey away from the earth and started its return. Thus the solstice became the occasion for celebration and a deep sigh of relief that the sun was not going away forever.

Christmas, the solstice's most current iteration, has been special to me all my life. If I had to pick one time to freeze-frame and extend into eternity, it would be Christmas Eve. In that moment, people everywhere can sense that a new dimension to life is about to be born.

The imagery of the solstice and Christmas, I think, gives us the right relationship between the dark and the light. It is the very fact that there is so much more darkness than light that makes celebrating the light so special. Darkness occupies the much larger portion of the universe; it gives birth to light, perhaps literally. Out of that great void, says physicist Brian Swimme, the very substance of the universe may be born. Scientifically, this means that matter is not just hiding out there somewhere in space, but is literally created out of what we see as nothingness (Swimme 1987). That nothingness, it may turn out, is actually an energy field, and substances themselves may be concentrations of energy. This would explain why I feel so strongly that I can sense the trees in the dark in a way that I cannot in the daylight.

Now we are in the arena of mystery, of glimpsing the secrets of the universe. The mystery, as Ray Bradbury says, is something that we can never solve, but only "climb over" and "finally, inhabit" (Zukav 1984). Inhabiting the mystery of the night, by simply standing outside under the stars, is exactly what I love to do. This experience calls forth a reverence and a profound love for that which is beyond my knowing, which light can partly illuminate but never fully penetrate.

This love I have for the night is my best defense against despair. The image of the pregnant promise in the apparent nothingness of darkness, like the earth that holds the seed of spring in her winter womb, is what makes the day-to-day dying and birthing in business and in life bearable. Women who have experienced the growth of a fetus within their own bodies know that the feminine is the keeper of the dark that enables birth. A counterpoint to masculine thinking, the feminine has less need to know exactly what is true on the outside and can live with more ambiguity, because life is stirring from within.

The cycles of life, then, are seen and experienced in two different ways. On the one hand, they are tumultuous and painful. On the other, they are the labor pains that produce new life and fundamentally new experiences, not only for individuals but for whole societies. My young nephew once said, after climbing a two-story ladder from a boat to the top of a very high pier for the second time, that being scared twice in one day was just about right. The challenge is finding the balance between safety and surrender to the frightening cycles that we have to endure for new learning to take place. What can help us to realize both in our lives is an environment in which we feel truly secure. In the next chapter, I talk about what that environment could be, an environment I am calling deep community.

Chapter 5

Deep Community

It is man's task, his greatest task, not to learn to love, but to learn to create the conditions in which love alights upon us and remains with us.

—IRENE CLAREMONT DE CASTILLEJO, *Knowing Woman: A Feminine Psychology*

Like "excellence," "empowerment," and "quality control," "community" has become a catchword of the 1990s. But to many it has an uncomfortable feminine feel to it, bringing up images of soft, fuzzy, feel-good sessions, artificially contrived. Community is nice, some might think, but I still have to pay the mortgage, so let's get real.

I believe that community already exists and is an important source of strength we can draw upon in all aspects of our lives, including business. The failure to recognize community interferes, it seems to me, with the success of any organization, business or otherwise. Furthermore, I suspect, our ability to draw sustenance from community may be exactly what will allow us to break through our greatest difficulties as a species.

I am using the phrase "deep community" to describe this phenomenon, which I believe already exists in nature. When we put the word "deep" in front of the word "ecology," we add a consciousness of the intangible depths of connection. Deep community means the same thing to me; it is community based on something that lies beneath the visible structures and processes of our society. Just as the beauty of the earth and its systems is there for us to take in fully if we are present to it, deep community does not have to be invented, but needs to be experienced and paid attention to.

The medieval mystic Meister Eckhart once said, "God is at home. It is we who have gone out for a walk" (Fox 1983, 15). Deep community is a lot like God in this respect. Similar to Eckhart's statement, Jeanne Borei of Creative Change Technologies, a corporate community-building consultant, told me that her voice teacher compared God to the "bass note" from which all the other notes and harmonies can be heard. "Try this on a piano some time," she continued. "Strike a low bass note and listen. Slowly you will hear all the other harmonies come into play. Deep community is like that. It is the foundation level for the rest of our lives, literally our home base."

This "at home" quality of deep community shows up when we stumble across an animal in the woods and find our sense of wonder evoked. I once asked a group of people in a workshop to remember a time when they had had such an encounter. They shifted in their seats, settled in, and one by one as each went back to some precious, private moment, his or her eyes brightened. They remembered the soulful meeting of eyes and every detail of the animal, however long ago the encounter occurred.

This same sense of wonder is keenly felt in the human community when a child is born, when someone is seriously ill, or when a natural disaster strikes. I remember well the Blizzard of '78 in Boston. All transportation stopped for a week. People went to heroic lengths that first night to get people out of their cars on the highway. Then, for days afterward, people came out—on foot, on makeshift snowshoes, on cross-country skis— and stopped to talk to anyone they met. In teams we shoveled out all the cars in our neighborhood. All the normal daily procedures were suspended. The energy and excitement—the fun—was out on the street helping with whatever was needed in the moment. If this experience of community is not a naturally productive part of our collective lives, why are we so good at it under such circumstances with so little practice?

Even while most of us are absorbed with the daily routine of jobs that consume forty or more hours per week, there is an ongoing background of deep community that holds our civil community together outside of its formal arrangements, making sure, for example, that old people get to the store or the hospital when they need to. This is the activity of care that women intuitively subscribe to and that men find increasingly satisfying too. This is the domain of family reunions, of volunteer fire fighting and emergency medical services, of church suppers, and of volunteer hospital, library, and school workers. For those who know they have made a real difference in other people's lives in this way, the awe they feel about their experience is just as real as the awe I feel when I see an animal in the wild.

Many of us who are now in our fifties relegated all of this type of work to the realms of the unskilled when we were in our twenties. We felt it was unimportant, and we disdained it as full-time work. Instead we left our hometowns and went off to college to get ourselves ready to save the world through our brilliant ideas and sophisticated management skills. But now a lot of us are finding our way back to community work wherever we have landed. We find we need the nourishment this work gives to our lives. At midlife, I am hearing both women and men question the wisdom of pursuing the full-time careers they were so sure they wanted when they were younger. They aren't *really* wanting to give it all up, but they are asking some critically important questions about what constitutes a meaningful and productive life.

In addition to the personal nourishment individuals derive from immersing themselves in community work, our society gains immeasurably from this invisible and unpaid infrastructure, as many working women know intimately. They may work all day at their public job, but these women are never far from their private job of family caretaking. My sister Jean, who is a pediatric nurse practitioner, reports that, by and large, it is still the women who leave the office to care for a sick school-age child or an aging parent.

If this undercurrent of connection and care is so important and so satisfying in our personal lives, how could it possibly not be important and satisfying in our public lives?

DISCONNECTION AND RECONNECTION

Deep community is not a luxury. People suffer major negative affects when it is missing. To see this, we have only to look at the chaos in our urban environments and in those places around the world where the fabric of society is being torn apart. But we could also look closer to home at the stress we feel in our own work lives. When I am disconnected from deep community, I experience a free-floating fear. My individual nature, which is introverted and intuitive—in a world in which most successful businesspeople are extroverted and concrete—is a part of the story, but not the whole of it. I experience this fear at random, not just associated with actual circumstances, and I know this fear has been hidden behind my outward optimism all my life. I am far less concerned by the thought that some particular business project will not work out than I am concerned by the presence of a kind of black despair that the world expects me to fail, even relishes that failure, or worse, that it is profoundly indifferent to my welfare. This sense of profound indifference is the absence of community.

This fear is different from the fear one normally and appropriately feels when challenged to go beyond one's current limits and knowledge. It is a fear associated with not feeling safe in the body. The body is the source of enormous vulnerability. On the simplest level, when the body does not get enough food, water, and shelter, it does not survive. But on a far more sinister level, the body is susceptible to the most vile forms of abuse. History is full of evidence of this. Ironically, when people contemptuously describe other human beings as animals, they are describing patterns of violence against the body that occur more often among our own species than among others. Animals kill what they need for food and to protect themselves, but rarely do they prolong the killing for pleasure or to experience the power gained by torturing another living being. There have been no inquisitions among other animal species of which I am aware. Nor to my knowledge have animals ever sent waves of their young males to their death in wars to preserve power, or systematically raped the females of another clan, as we saw in the conflict between the Serbs, Croats, and Muslims in Bosnia. Being a human being in the society of other human beings is not a safe business; on the contrary, it can be extremely dangerous. Although I don't have to live with the atrocities that we see human beings inflicting upon each other around the globe, I do have the uncomfortable feeling that the same failure to experience deep community with others underlies the indifference I feel in modern organizations, just in a less extreme form.

We could actually learn a lot about the presence of deep community from other animal species. They instinctually know how to live collectively yet spontaneously in such a way that the burden of providing for physical needs does not have to be carried alone or occupy all of one's time. Extensive hoarding over years does not seem to be necessary for most of them.

We think that our lives are categorically better than the lives of animals or our fellow human beings living a century ago. In many respects we are right, but not completely. Many of us still work forty to sixty hours a week at jobs we don't like. We worry constantly about losing what we have or about being unable to build a secure retirement in a country that has mandatory social security. When do we get time just to live?

Sometimes I wish I were a wolf, knowing myself to be part of a pack, and counting instinctually on support from that quarter. If I could truly feel myself to be so connected, I would be much more at ease in this world, the natural dangers of life in the wild not withstanding. I would certainly be more at ease at work if I felt connected in this way to other people. This image I have of a pack reminds me of a dream I had in which I was on a submarine with many other people. There was illness and trauma, and many did not recover, but everyone was comforted because everyone was in physical contact with someone, even if it was only a hand reaching across a bunk to give solace. No one was suffering *unnecessarily*, I thought with relief and comfort as I awoke, and that was the critical word for me—"unnecessarily."

Recently my husband told me an interesting story about the procedure for rescuing horses from trailers that have overturned on the highway. One goes into the trailer and sits on the horses' heads; it is the only thing that calms them. In the human sphere one offers a similar kind of comfort in the aftermath of an automobile accident. An emergency medical technician (EMT) goes into the car and, in addition to providing medical assessment and care, sits with the victim explaining what is happening while the rescue crew cuts the car away. It is the human touch that matters—both the reassuring touch of the EMT's skilled hands on the victim's body and the comfort of his or her voice that conveys experience and empathy.

The comfort of being part of a pack, then, would not protect me from either disaster or death, nor hard work, but it would diminish my fear and free up considerable energy to be put to better use. One of the great paradoxes of deep community—and a great opportunity for business—is that experiencing the inner strength that deep community gives us makes us capable of our greatest autonomous action. War, ironically, is a great example; veterans report that during battle a soldier is never more connected to his comrades nor more totally on his own.

This experience of a human animal connection and mutual reverence for our animal bodies and the body of the earth is what I was unconsciously craving when I moved to the country. I wanted to see if the familiarity that comes from knowing people over a long period of time, and dealing together with what nature gives out in one specific place, would make a difference. I imagined that it could be like Wendell Berry's exquisite novel,

A Place on Earth, in which he describes the depth of life in one small community with immense, though subtle compassion and with not one unnecessary word.

I have not been disappointed by country life, but I have been humbled. It has been harder than I anticipated to shed the protective layers of cheery autonomy that are so much a part of middle-class culture. I have internalized this modern American middle-class ethic of autonomy and mobility well—so well that it is not easy to work my way back to the more instinctual activity of care that my mother and mother's mother lived in daily. But here in the country I have observed people doing what I find so hard to do. Despite the reputation rural people have for preferring to die rather than ask for help, when help is really needed, it is given and received instantly and less self-consciously than in the middle-class suburbs where I have lived.

This is not because rural people live in some kind of nostalgic utopia of the past. The simple reality of life itself seems to me to be more deeply valued here on a day-to-day basis. People here are connected to place—the hills and valleys, the snow in winter, the stars at night, the flowers in the meadow, the river. As Wendell Berry says of his character Old Jack, "He believed that people could have no devotion to each other that they did not give at the same time to the place they had in common" (Berry 1975, 185). There *does* seem to be a connection between loving the body of the earth, accepting ourselves as an animal species dependent on that body and each other, and truly loving ourselves. Among the conditions "in which love can alight upon us and remain with us" seems to be a positive connection to place and to the people in that place. Love that "remains with us," as Claremont de Castillejo describes it, is really what I mean by deep community (Claremont de Castillejo, 1973, 125).

THE DISCOMFORT WITH COMMUNITY IN PUBLIC LIFE

While we all live in community in some respects daily, our conscious understanding of it is still very fuzzy. In my mind there are two important ingredients involved in consciously experiencing deep community. First is a feeling of spontaneous appreciation—dare I say a *sacred regard*—for those who are in my community, just as I feel sacred regard for an animal in the wild. When I experience deep community, I feel that sacred regard for everyone, even if I don't particularly like them. Second is the experience of place as part of my community—the place where I am living, working, or meeting. This has been true for me in my childhood neighborhood, my campus dormitory and grounds, my first apartment in the city, and every space in which I have ever worked.

It is hard for modern mobile people to accept the fact that place is an ingredient of community, because we move around so often that it is difficult to get truly connected to place. But as Bob Mang, a California businessman who has been involved with regional environmental planning for many years, wrote,

> It is important to understand that identity, so vital to an
> enduring community, springs from a common agreement about
> boundaries. . . . Modern corporations, constantly changing the
> places of their employees, owners and production, or
> "electronic communities" that share no place outside the mind,
> are not, and cannot be, sustainable communities. Both create
> bonds in different forms—one as an organization, the other as a
> network. Both bonds are undeniably valuable, but because they
> are not connected to place or nonhuman nature, they tap into
> only a part of our whole being" (Gozdz 1995, 335).

Furthermore the places where most of us must live in order to commute to our work sites are often devoid of the natural qualities that evoke a sense of the sacred.

As a species, we seem to have an inherent capacity to experience sacred regard for other people and for the earth. But I am deeply aware of my own inability to engage in a natural way with my new neighbors, giving and taking unself-consciously what I need and what I can give to others. There are certain boundaries of my cultural experience that I find hard to overcome, even when my instincts crave a new orientation. So, even knowing that deep community is "at home," as comforting as that is, and experiencing community within my most intimate circles of friends and family, it is still an enormously difficult task to bring myself and others home to community in the public sphere. Even bringing up such issues in the workplace left me wondering if I were tough enough for business. If we craved deep community in the workplace, were we just a dysfunctional group, so needy individually that we would never be able to participate effectively in the adult economic world? It took me years of study and conversations with other obviously functional people to realize that something was missing in our perceptions of who we should be rather than in our individual development. Why is this so?

Our business culture—really all of our public life—is built on a systems theory within which our deepest experience of community is largely *invisible*. That systems theory is the abstract, contractual foundation of our whole American legal system. Having left European countries where human social and economic relationships were governed by class membership and more rigid ideas about appropriate human behavior than we would accept, our ancestors rightly developed a system that spelled out in far more detail than had been done before what a government *couldn't* do to interfere with an individual life. Our system is brilliantly built on our belief in individual freedom. Its cornerstones are restraint from interference, fairness, and a practice of writing down our collective agreements so that all parties are clear about both their rights and their responsibilities.

This system is so good that we expect it to handle every aspect of our social relationships, which it cannot possibly do. The most obvious example of this expectation is the crisis in our medical care system. A doctor is trained to give a patient treatment that will provide the best opportunity for that patient to recover and live a healthy life. Instead he/she is increasingly fearful of trying something that is experimental or of withholding any available treatment that promises a possible cure, even where intuition and good judgment suggest it is inappropriate.

To do so would set the doctor up for liability. Because of these dynamics, frustrated patients, who have experienced the expense, pain, and often the indignity of an impersonal and highly technical health care system can become cynical and, it seems to me, more inclined to sue as a way of getting some satisfaction. Collectively we are so frustrated by the skyrocketing cost of health care that we are trying, through our government, to control medical procedures in a *contractual* way that adds mountains of paperwork for our already overworked practitioners. Thus we feed a vicious cycle in which pressure builds to move the doctor away from, not toward, engaging with the real desires and needs of the patient in decisions about treatment. Angrily we accuse medical people of greed and lack of caring. But for many doctors, their youthful ideals of human service have been deeply damaged by a system that limits their freedom to make courageous and wise decisions on behalf of their individual patients.

As good as it is, our legal, contractual system cannot generate the *sacred regard* for others that spontaneously appears in healthy families, among close friends, or, on a larger scale, during a natural disaster like the Blizzard of '78 or the recent floods in the midwestern United States. Sacred regard for other beings, which is the foundation of deep community, must be more than just a concept. It has to be *experienced* as it was in the above crises. The trick is to figure out how to integrate that experience into our routine daily lives.

Just as the word "amoral" does not mean the same thing as "immoral," contractual business is not necessarily hostile to community, but it does not foster it. The system itself is neutral. Our legal system goes a long way toward protecting us from the worst damage we can do to one another, but it does not have the capacity to teach us kindness and sacred regard. Even in my small rural community, whose virtues I have extoled throughout this book, during political conflicts we revert to the same mean-spiritedness and rancor that people struggle with everywhere.

The spontaneous feminine affirmation of life, which is the basis from which we recognize and value deep community, is missing in our institutions. We have far clearer and more conscious standards for ensuring competence in terms of productivity than we do for developing competence in human relatedness. A friend who recently initiated some business in Russia told me that two of his Russian contacts said that they thought the feminine archetype was dead in the United States. Although I cannot be sure exactly what they meant by that, this statement from outside our culture seemed to me to underlie what I have been saying—which is that our public culture has no real place for the feminine activity of care that goes beyond the exercise of restraint and fairness and that works toward the building of sacred regard for each other.

The appearance of women in large numbers in business and political life has stirred the waters and raised some consciousness. But mostly women have been struggling to master the masculine culture of focused consciousness, productivity, and contractual relationships. There is still no conscious awareness of deep community in our public institutions. If there were, we would not let our media trash the private lives of individuals who inhabit those institutions, nor would we tolerate the countless injuries we inflict on each other in the local political arena.

As more women work longer hours at the office, they have actually taken away some of the feminine energy that has historically sustained our out-of-work and outside-of-politics communities. This is not something for women to feel guilty about, but something they are struggling with, because the public sphere needs feminine energy as surely as the private sphere does. We are, I hope, in the vortex of powerful changes, the birthing of a new standard for relatedness that we can only glimpse, but to which women—and men who are conscious of and value the feminine—are, even now, making important contributions.

THE IMPORTANCE OF DEEP COMMUNITY IN BUSINESS

How can the sacred regard of deep community contribute in a substantial way to business culture? On the most basic level, a sense of deep community restrains us from doing harm to those with whom we feel connected, whether we like them personally or not. We know this already in both our business lives and our personal lives, and we know that this restraint is fundamentally different from the restraint of law. If there were not widespread cultural agreement against certain destructive behavior patterns such as killing, our legal system would be hard pressed to contain such behavior.

On a higher level, deep community leads us to a greater appreciation of each other, to the mutual sacred regard that gives us a greater sense of ultimate safety. Within this sphere of increased safety, we can tell more of our own truth without fearing that we will be, figuratively, killed. Sacred regard increases our sense of our own value and gives us room to explore our capabilities.

Earlier I said that a paradox of deep community is that it can give us the strength to engage in the most autonomous activity of our lives, and I cited wartime comradeship as an example. Another surprising example comes from a team-building exercise used in a Fortune 500 company. The exercise involved a "magic carpet" made up of square carpet tiles that were wired in such a way that an invisible maze could be created. The task of each team was to find its way through the maze with the fewest mistakes. Stepping on the wrong square a first time didn't count as a mistake, but when a second member of the team made the same mistake, team members forfeited some portion of the imaginary sum of money they were given at the beginning of the game. Each minute they spent working on the exercise also cost the team imaginary money, so the object was to get across the floor as fast as possible with the minimum number of mistakes. The consultant who led this exercise reported to the Fortune 500 trainees that of all the groups she had worked with using this exercise, the quickest had been a group of nuns, because they were not afraid of making mistakes! Now if there was ever a group of people oriented toward deep community and away from rugged individualism, I would have to guess that it would be a group of nuns!

We need experiences like the maze game, preferably from real life rather than from training situations, so we can see that the experience of deep community can actually enhance individual achievement. If they haven't yet seen that such a value exists, it will be difficult for many people to push through their concerns that experiencing community at work will make us too soft. Will making community a conscious reality in business force us into a cushy "both-and" mentality, leaving us no room for discrimination or the "either-or" aspect of life? The trick is to rigorously include that capacity for discrimination as part of our "*both* both-and *and* either-or" mind-set, so we can expand our business thinking without sacrificing the strengths that have been acquired by centuries of refining our focused consciousness.

One way to begin embracing community in business would be to distinguish between "everyone belongs" and "I love everybody," the latter being what so many people expect when they think of community as a soft, unrealizable ideal. "I love everybody" implies a level of intimacy that is not necessarily appropriate at work. As I have learned from participating in many community-building groups, "everyone belongs" means that I respect each person's authentic value, but I do not have to be intimate with everyone. The word "authentic" stems from the word "author," and it has to do with being genuine, with conforming to fact. Does the way I behave, the way I present myself, conform to the reality of my nature? "Intimate," on the other hand, has to do with "making known" that which is innermost, private, personal. That which is intimate, we would assume, would also be authentic, but not all that is authentic must be intimate.

This confusion between intimacy and authenticity can be a serious problem in business when it leads us to want every person to reveal everything about him or herself. It is important to be authentic and to appreciate the authenticity of others, so that we can each make the best contribution we can to the task of the community. But a person does not have to reveal the deep, dark secrets of childhood in the workplace. This is the difference between authenticity and intimacy.

We have for so long kept so much of ourselves hidden at work that having the opportunity to express our authentic selves in that environment can be exhilarating. We want everyone to have the same experience, but being one's authentic self is different for different people. In the sexual revolution of the 1960s, for example, you were not regarded as liberated in some circles if you didn't try everything with almost everybody. That unwritten requirement was as oppressive as not being able to try anything at all, and the same idea applies in community. It is important, therefore, to be very clear about when a person's participation in a process at work is needed to accomplish the task of the organization and when it really is not. It is easy to put our own spin on this, as I might have done in the case of my production manager to whose behavior the women in my office objected. I could have made an issue of his conflict with the women and insisted that he change his way of relating and working, but was that necessary for the health of the group and for my company? He really did do his job well, and he never failed to share the information other people needed to do their jobs well. And he never hid who he was or demanded that others be the same.

If authenticity is a key attribute of deep community, women as mothers have practical experience to offer. On a day-to-day basis, mothering involves the application of the feminine capacity to see and appreciate the uniqueness of individuals and to facilitate the interaction of people with conflicting styles and strengths. While women sometimes have difficulty asking for what they need themselves; they are getting better at doing so, and they can be fierce in the defense of others. Women are also a quick study when it comes to backing off from rigid positions, positions that insist that community must conform to a particular construct.

What we all need to do more than anything else—women and men alike—is strengthen our consciousness of the ultimate capacity of deep community to increase self-esteem and thus creativity and productivity in our organizations. Then we need to give more credence to our capacity for presence and being, which will help more with the subtleties of experiencing deep community than all the concepts and principles in the world.

Our capacity for presence and being is especially important when we reach an impasse. Acquiring and using power over other people is still the normal way that people get what they want—in business and in the world at large—and we are a long way from any significant change on that score. Working through community issues with a person with a strictly "either-or" mind-set demands everything we can muster, sometimes more.

This situation reminds me of Psyche's second task on the journey of feminine mastery. She has to get some wool from the golden fleece of some very powerful rams. A reed by the river coaches her not to expose herself to the rams in the open field in the fierce noonday sun. If she will just wait until dusk when the rams are asleep, she can go to a nearby grove and collect wisps of the rams' wool that have been caught there on the branches (Neumann 1990).

Somewhere in this myth is a clue to appropriate action in the face of the ruthless and destructive side of masculine energy, which the rams represent. I can only hope that by staying true to our instincts for deep community, and digging deep for the sacred regard we have even for those people whom we find the most difficult, we will someday get the insights that will lead us to break through our most difficult conflicts without breaking each other. If we can find the way to resolve the most difficult conflicts in public life, as we have done for centuries in caring for our families, we could transform the world we live in. Resolving conflicts of this magnitude is a tall order, some would say utopian, but I cannot believe that people really want to fight wars or abuse each other, in business or anywhere else, if we can find a viable alternative.

Once realized, deep community, as those who have experienced it—in marriage, in families, with friends, in nature—

know, offers rewards that surpass almost everything else that we crave. With deep community together we can bring to our public organizations a new approach that is neither too soft for good decision making nor injurious to the bottom line. We need to keep naming this experience of deep community for ourselves and for others so that it becomes conscious and usable in business. A conscious experience of deep community is what will help us eventually diminish and, I hope, eliminate the unnecessary fear and stress that blocks our creativity and productivity in the workplace. It can also give us more room for courageous acts of conscience when we are up against the wall of our own survival.

SUMMING UP

In this section, I have identified four aspects of the feminine principle that I believe can have a powerful impact on the workplace. The first, diffuse awareness, is the mental capacity to perceive reality with the breadth and scope of a field, such that the underlying relationships between things can be seen and fully appreciated.

Diffuse awareness is underscored by the core feminine value that deeply affirms and appreciates life itself. This feminine affirmation of life allows us to respond spontaneously in the moment and communicates itself through presence and being. I believe that increasing our experience of presence and being—here and now, in this world—can be a major source of healing for our human tendency to mentally split spirit and matter. This mental split has created tension within the human species for centuries and, in my mind, it is at the heart of our troubled relationship with the earth.

A third aspect of the feminine principle is the capacity to accept the cycles of life, always holding in mind the ultimate integrity of life, so that we can let go of habits that are not in our long-term interest.

And finally, the recognition of deep community is what makes it possible for us to feel secure enough to surrender to the cycles of life that are required of us for new growth. I believe that as a species we must master a conscious awareness of deep community in all our institutions as the ultimate means by which we can resolve conflict and break through our long history of violence and war.

Keeping these four aspects of the feminine principle in mind, Part 2 will look at some feminine patterns of behavior in the workplace that illustrate more concretely how the feminine principle can and does play out in our daily work lives.

Part 2

Feminine Patterns of Work

Chapter 6

Organizing Information and Action

Over the past several years I've developed the habit of using index cards to record the facts uncovered in the course of an investigation. I pin the cards on the bulletin board that hangs above my desk, and in idle moments I arrange and rearrange the data according to no known plan. At some point I realize how different a detail can look when it's seen out of context. Like the pieces of a jigsaw puzzle, the shape of reality seems to shift according to circumstance. What seems strange or unusual can make perfect sense when it's placed in the proper setting. By the same token, what seems unremarkable can suddenly yield up precious secrets when placed against a different backdrop."

—KINSEY MILLHONE from SUE GRAFTON's *K Is for Killer*

Kinsey Millhone, Sue Grafton's fictitious private investigator, is one of my favorite characters. Though she will tell you over and over again that she hates nature, she is a very down-to-earth person with no pretenses (although she *is* a very good liar). Her description of how she sorts the facts in her cases offers us a very good analogy for the way in which the feminine naturally sorts information (Grafton 1995).

You can probably already see the relationship between this sorting process and diffuse awareness. It makes sense that when we take in information in a broad, diffuse way, we will sort information that way as well. There are no preconceived categories in Kinsey's system. She just puts the details up on her bulletin board and looks to see what might be related to what. She keeps switching the details around at random until some pattern reveals itself.

SORTING SEEDS

Similarly, if we go back to the Psyche and Eros myth, we can see that the ants representing Psyche's feminine instincts are doing the same thing. Starting with the seeds themselves, the ants sorted them according to the characteristics they found in the individual seeds. This one is brown, and this one is gray. This one is large, this one small. This one is coarse, and this one smooth. You might say that brown or gray, large or small, coarse or smooth are concepts. But they are concepts that come out of, rather than dictate the process. The ants start with all of what is there in an unorganized heap, and the categories for sorting are derived from the substances themselves and include all the seeds that are present, even if there is a one-of-a-kind category. This is a very different activity from ordering information when you have already been told what the categories should be—tree seeds, for example, or vegetable seeds, or flower seeds.

The most powerful example of this process occurred for me when I started to assemble this book. The image of sorting seeds became indelibly etched in my brain in September of 1994. I came across a paper that I had written for a group of women friends, and remembered what had been happening in my life when I wrote that paper five years earlier. At that time I was full of new ideas; I was reading Jungian depth psychology, the new science, and creation spirituality literature. I was also participating in the Beyond War movement, where I found a group of extraordinary people, many of whom had had very successful business careers, giving their time and energy to shifting the world's paradigm about war in a profoundly good-spirited rather than a confrontational way. It was a magical time during which I experienced a serendipitous converging of all the work I had done over the years in my marriage, in my personal reading, and in my business life.

Although that earlier period couldn't have been as perfect as I remembered it to be, it certainly had a numinous or spiritual quality. When I looked back in 1994, I wondered where my faith and hope had gone in the intervening five years. The root of the paper I had written for my friends had been the Psyche and Eros myth. Rereading that paper, I saw something for the first time: all the energy in my writing had centered on Psyche's recognition of Eros, her discovery of the divine masculine. Barely a word did I write about the consequence of that encounter: Eros fled. As Psyche held the oil lamp above to see her lover, some oil spilled and burned him. So, in physical pain, and in a rage that she had violated their agreement that he would only come to her in the dark, Eros vanished.

In my business experience, and particularly in my immersion in the work of the Beyond War movement, I had indeed seen glimpses of the divine masculine in the high purpose and brilliant skill of many people, particularly men, whom I met. That was the point in my life when I shifted my focus from the wounds of being female in this society to the opportunities for exquisite collaboration with the masculine both within myself and in the external world. But I was still largely in awe of the "other."

What I had failed to notice when I read that myth was that at the same time that Psyche became conscious of her feminine capacity to love the divine masculine, she was separated from her beloved. Just by becoming conscious of Eros, she offended him. From the vantage point of her intense love for Eros, this is an incomprehensible turn of events, but in the end the process leads to a more complete feminine development. At this point in the myth, Psyche had to engage in the four grueling tasks that would lead her to real feminine mastery. Only after completing these tasks could she reconnect with Eros on an equal footing and become a goddess in her own right. (Meanwhile, we may presume, Eros had his own developmental work to do!)

Perhaps, I thought in 1994, it was time to reread the story of the tasks. And that is what brought me back to the sorting of the seeds, Psyche's first task. Over the next year, I culled through ten years of journals and correspondence, picked a seed of an idea here and worked with it, then picked another one there. Like Kinsey Millhone, I sometimes lifted whole paragraphs or whole essays from one place and pasted them via computer with others without the slightest idea what the connection would turn out to be. I ended up with twenty-one essays, which I linked and relinked in myriad ways. It wasn't until I engaged with some publishers that I brought my focused consciousness skills back into action and assembled the book in the form that you see it now.

What is important about my process is that I could not have written this book any other way. Had I started to write from a conceptual outline, the book would have been sterile and dead, if it had ever gotten written at all, because I had not yet revealed to myself the real content I wished to express.

I have gone nearly crazy judging myself in business situations when I find myself sorting information in the way I have just described. But I do it all the time. A project is not real for me until I grasp the categories that emerge from sorting the individual pieces. For instance, when writing job descriptions and developing organizational charts, I needed to know what people had to say about what they really did, and I had to get a sense of what they *loved* to do. Sometimes this took a long, convoluted conversation, or several such long, convoluted conversations, until we realized what a person's work really entailed. I found it difficult to stick with this process, and sometimes I short-circuited myself, because the process seemed to take up more time than it was *supposed* to take.

I have always been happy—actually relieved—to get an organizational chart done. But no organizational chart has even contained what is most alive to me about people's jobs. It is easier for me to feel connected to my employees, customers, and vendors if I can hold in my mind the whole picture—which comes to me through my diffuse awareness—of what matters to them and what they feel responsible for than it is for me tell you exactly what they do.

This method of sorting information has an amorphous quality to it. It requires keeping the whole field of thought open, holding conclusions and categories lightly, and living with tension and paradox. This is the painstaking and necessary *activity* associated with the feminine capacity for diffuse awareness: a continuous sorting of the ever-shifting seeds of reality.

By just about anyone's standards, we live in troubled times and face some enormous problems that our current view of economic reality shows no signs of being able to solve. By repeatedly bringing into the dialogue those questions that come at us from the periphery, from the seeds of information for which no categories yet exist in our business charts and calculations, we may work our way to effective solutions. Many of these categories are already somewhat known but primarily conceptually: such things as the damage we do to the earth that does not show up in the expense columns of our corporate profit and loss statements, or the disturbing sight of homeless people in the city who have no viable way to enter the economy. The task is to sort and to continue to sort—against the odds of finding a way to deal with these problems—until we learn how we can work into our current structures what does not now fit. This work is like a long-term marriage, living for decades day to day with another person and working through all the nitty-gritty problems that arise. More of the answers come from the years of slow and deliberate experimentation than from sudden big insights.

Not long ago at a yard sale I came across an old book entitled *SEEDS: The Yearbook of Agriculture, 1961.* Instinctively I picked it up and started to read. "Good seeds," wrote then Secretary of Agriculture Orville Freeman in the foreword, "can be a means of bringing about an Age of Plenty and an Age of Peace and Freedom. We can use good seeds to help end hunger and fear. . . . So used, our seeds can be more meaningful to a hungry world than can the rocket that first put man on the moon." He wrote literally, of course, but I am reading this metaphorically. The feminine instinct to see and sort all the seeds of life may be as important to our future as the literal seeds that we plant in the ground. "Seeds are many things," the text of the book began. "Above all else, they are a way of survival of their species. They are a way by which embryonic life can be almost suspended and then revived to new development" (U.S. Department of Agriculture 1961, 1).

WOMEN'S WAYS OF WORKING

In the myth of Psyche and Eros, the ants are the creatures capable of the kind of work it takes to sort seeds. It is interesting, therefore, to look at what ants actually *do*. Some gather food for their colony; while others care for the young, and still others protect those who are gathering food. Those who work on food gathering excavate miles of tunnels and build roads, sometimes even arching them over. They will work in chains, dropping materials to others below to save energy. And there are a lot of them, all doing pretty much the same thing. We very rarely think of ants individually, but when we do, we often think of each of them carrying a load that is heavy compared to the weight of its body. Interestingly, the ants join forces to carry an item that is too heavy for one alone, and in a crisis they communicate with each other down the line. If one is injured, others will rush to the rescue.

There is a lot about this scenario that reminds me of women working together. Even the most independent of women do not seem to mind much that others are doing parallel work. If women were not working in a business culture where individual achievement is so highly valued, would many of them really care about specific ownership of their ideas or accomplishments? My sense is that most women want to be acknowledged for carrying their weight more than for their independence of thought or action. But in a world of copyrights, titles, and bonuses, singling oneself out is essential to getting any acknowledgment at all.

I said earlier that for two thousand years we have been developing and perfecting focused consciousness, and I asked what else is needed to make life work that would serve not as a substitute for hunter-warrior consciousness but could work as its partner. We can begin to see an answer in the way in which many women think about themselves and work together. Vera Brittain reports that her friend Winifred Holtby said of her life, "I never feel like I've had a life of my own. My existence seems to me like a clear stream which has simply reflected other people's stories and problems" (Brittain 1940, 1). Some may interpret this to mean that women fail to see themselves as the center of their own lives as men do. Yet I am wondering whether an image of oneself as a "clear stream" is a symbol of a special kind of ego strength, equal to the heroic image. And I am attracted to this image of water generally, as I am attracted to the image of the ants.

I have often had the feeling when working with a group of women to accomplish a task that we were just swimming together. This experience can be especially pleasurable when the work is physical, like assembling papers for a presentation or a mass mailing, or working together in communal cooking; but it also happens when we are creating ideas or products. I remember well when, as a high school teacher in the 1970s, I met with a group of women faculty members to design a program to implement Massachusetts' Title IX legislation to generate educational equity. It was obvious in our very first meeting that just being together to work on any project was a blissful respite for us from the normal pattern of daily classes.

Working together like this does not feel like merging, but more like floating together in a much larger field; there is an actual sensation of flowing. This kind of flow can drive organizational designers crazy; you cannot artificially stimulate it, nor can you stop it without feeling like you are literally damming something up.

MAINTENANCE AND ORCHESTRATION IN TIMES OF CHANGE

Besides being pleasurable, what can this fluid feminine pattern of working offer to the business culture as a whole? It is interesting to note that the word "economy" actually derives from a combination of *"oikos"*, which means "house," and *"nemein"*, which means "to manage"—the science of household management, then, on a very large scale. Besides the structural side of a household, and the assigned roles, there are also wild combinations of characteristics of households such as busy, vital, contradictory, sustaining, diverse, organic, noisy, interactive, colorful, close, funny, frightening, warm, spontaneous, loving, conflicted, happy, angry, abusive, and safe. This is not the stuff of organizational charts, but it is the stuff with which women are familiar and at home.

A recent issue of *Forbes* featured eight widows who had known little of their husbands' businesses, but who successfully took over when their husbands died unexpectedly. Each woman used what she knew from running a household to assess the business and pull it out of a downward spiral or build it further. "People think being a housewife doesn't give you any experience, but we learn how to manage our time, our children, our husbands," said Irma Elder, who now runs Troy Motors in Michigan (revenues $370 million). "Earnings were down, expenses up. You don't need a genius to tell you what to do. Cut costs," said Loida Lewis, who took over TLC Beatrice. "In many ways," she continued, "it is just a transposition (from household management to business.) Except that instead of dealing with

$100, there are now eight or nine zeroes there" (*Forbes*, November 20, 1995, 149–150).

Maintenance of organizations, or the management of the ongoing flow of human energy and resources, is an important part of business and one to which feminine energy is well suited. In our minds we associate maintenance with drudgery; it brings up images of thankless work that depletes the soul. But is it really? The Latin origin of "maintenance," *manu* and *tenere*, means "to hold in the hand." I would like to reconceptualize the importance of maintenance in our global household to include a dynamic feminine component that is more like orchestration of activity than the passive or static holding in place.

One of the most impressive executive "maintainers" I have known once said that men's stories around the campfire are almost always heroic. They are individual stories, calling upon heroes specifically by name, recounting the courage of the past and inspiring courage for the future. Men, this female executive hypothesized, have always run the majority of individual risks in society. But when the situation gets *too* risky—when the maintenance of society is jeopardized—women collectively step in and take over.

Now you can read this in a stereotypical way or question its historical accuracy, or you can see it as an interesting image of a dynamic in which both masculine and feminine energy play a necessary part in life. The woman telling this story was competent and self-possessed, a highly respected senior manager. She was unabashed in her acceptance of herself as a maintainer. Maintenance for her meant developing an organizational structure that really worked for both people and productivity in what she perceived, as I do also, as extremely turbulent times. Her strategy was to engage the whole company in an ongoing process of meshing their best energy and skills in a dynamic and constructive, yet no-nonsense way. Her work *was* orchestration. It had nothing in common with the compartmentalization of people into the organizational charts that are so typical of corporate pyramids.

When I think of the difference between this kind of orchestration and the many stories I have heard about men who have heroically built and led their companies, I am reminded of watching my nieces and nephews in action. My niece, who is the oldest, is like a little general in many ways, quick and decisive and totally at ease directing people to do thus and so. Her younger brother is far more mellow and easygoing by nature and is often the foot soldier carrying out her directives. Yet on the playground, to my amazement, I saw him launch easily into loud shouting matches with his peers over who was stronger, who was in charge, and what kind of consequences there would be if another boy dared challenge his position. Similarly, his cousins, two boys with very different personalities, engaged very naturally in turf battles. On the beach one day, one boy very calmly took a stick and drew a line between himself and his younger brother. "That side is yours," he explained, "and this is mine, and each goes around the world to the other side in China."

From these two experiences I learned that turf control and bossiness are not the same. They are the extremes of two orientations toward producing an outcome, and each follows a very different path. Once again, I want to be sure we do not look at this difference as "either-or." One is not right while the other is wrong.

I will be forever grateful to the consultant who took me aside when I tried to intervene between my partner and our sales manager. The consultant explained to me that their apparent hostility toward each other did not really mean anything but was a natural way for them to work through their differences. Since that time I have stayed out of the way of these kinds of confrontations between men. In the same way, I think men can learn to get out of the way when women are effectively orchestrating the individual energy that they find in their companies. This is maintenance of the best kind, holding human potential in one's hands and encouraging it to manifest itself in healthy, life-enhancing ways for the people and the organization involved. From a masculine perspective this process can seem disorderly, even chaotic, but the real evaluation of its merit should be based on what such orchestration produces. Since we tend to devalue this process we are a long way from having enough data to measure its potential effectiveness in business.

Many of us, however, know from personal experience just how effective a good orchestrator can be in business. In the late 1980s I coordinated a newspaper campaign for a nonprofit organization. Even more than for our regular clients, we had to be sensitive to the needs of volunteer workers who did not understand the complications of producing both copy and finished artwork for the ads. To delay the appearance of an ad for even one day would create enormous disappointment for the volunteers, in addition to getting us behind schedule in a time-sensitive political campaign. I was working on the East Coast placing the advertising in New England papers. The account executive for the agency that was producing the content and the finished artwork was in Los Angeles. The decision makers at the nonprofit agency were largely in San Francisco, but others were scattered around the country. For each of the four ads, the agency first developed the concept, then filled in the detailed copy as the deadline approached. Through a conference call, we approved the final copy, and then the account executive and I went into action.

What she had to do was monitor the progress of the copywriting, the copy production, and the express delivery of the final product to several newspapers. What I had to do was supervise communication with the newspapers if a delivery was not made or if it was going to arrive later than we had expected.

This may seem pretty straightforward, but it definitely was not. At her end, copywriters would get creative blocks or get sidetracked on other crisis projects, or the production staff would get backed up so that they could not produce an ad by a predetermined deadline. At my end, parcels got lost and newspaper publishers got panicky about deadlines, so I found myself coaxing reluctant delivery systems into action and talking news-paper salespeople into accepting delivery at the eleventh hour.

With so many things that could go wrong, it would have been no surprise if the account executive and I had been at odds with each other by the end of the month during which we worked together, but I have never seen so many potential fiascos diverted with virtually no rancor. And that was because the account executive in Los Angeles was the consummate orchestrator. She anticipated every possible problem and called me immediately if she even *thought* a deadline might be missed. That gave me the opportunity to devise a backup plan and communicate with the volunteers in the field. It also gave me the chance to tell her what was really critical—what we could live with and what would wreak havoc somewhere else in the system. I do not remember one instance in which we blamed each other or tried to pressure each other into doing something that was impossible for either of us to do. We had complete faith that the other would do everything possible to produce what was really needed. And all of this occurred by telephone, after only one face-to-face meeting in Los Angeles.

Good orchestrators produce miracles, not by creating fear of reprisals but by making people *want* to deliver for them. This most often occurs because the orchestrator is the first to give, thus modeling what is possible in terms of respect and open and honest communication, and also because such an orchestrator is rarely interested in laying blame. The pleasure is in finding a creative way to bypass the inevitable roadblocks and substitute a new channel for one that has broken down.

Because I doubted my ability to be forceful enough when faced with a conflict, it took me a long time to understand that I produced good results in a different way in my own company. Our office environment gave people room to be real with each other, to work through their differences, and to express their pleasure and their pain. We were not always at peace with one another, and we were not always orderly, but we had plenty of energy, and we basically cared about one another, while producing good work for our clients. Once I became conscious of the environment I had fostered, I began to take a different kind of pride in the contribution I made to my company and to be able to let go of my inner demands that I be good at everything else.

A NEW UNDERSTANDING OF "COLLECTIVITY"

I remember with amusement the challenge that Margaret Miles made to us at a Harvard Divinity School lecture. She wanted someone to write a female equivalent of St. Augustine's *Confessions*. As a group of us left the hall we brainstormed about this. "Well, for starters," said one of the members of our group, "it wouldn't be just one confession. It would be a collective anthology."

Women have developed a unique ability to work collectively—without any of the drudgery or rigidity that comes to mind when we think of what "the collective" means in communist or socialist theory. Women were working collectively in community activities long before Marx developed his theory, long before women entered the modern workforce, and long before anyone invented the word "team." Today women bring that same dynamic into their work life, either as team members or as individual leaders orchestrating a group effort. By bringing this element of spontaneous collectivity into business, women can also open a new pathway for men who feel more affinity for this style of working.

Feminine patterns of organizing information and action can bring new life into organizations, not as substitutes for existing masculine patterns, but as complements to them. To have both masculine and feminine styles and energy patterns present in the business environment is what we need, I believe, if the workplace is to be "actually healthy" as opposed to "what merely appears to be living" (DePree 1987, 21). And healthy business is definitely what I am after. What else do we need for our business environments to be healthy? In the next chapter we will explore how two very strong feminine patterns—feeling and trust—can enhance the workplace.

Chapter 7

Deep Feeling and Radical Trust

What she craved, and really felt herself entitled to, was a situation in which the noblest attitude should also be the easiest.

—EDITH WHARTON on LILY BART in *The House of Mirth*

Lily Bart is a mirror image of myself! I found it excruciating to read this novel because, like Lily, I so want the noble path to be easy. But if progress comes through dying and birthing, it is as often accompanied by heartbreak and sorrow as it is by joy and ecstasy.

Women cry. They cry when they are grieving. They cry when they are happy. They cry when they are angry—at least *I* do. This is a major inconvenience in business, but that actually tells us more about business than it does about women. Neither emotion nor weeping are signs of weakness. Tear ducts are designed by nature to cleanse the eye of foreign material and to cleanse the body of intense feeling, to wash it through. Surrendering to emotion and to tears is a lot like vomiting. After you have given in to it and feel your body's equilibrium restored, you wonder why you fought it so hard to begin with. But we always do. This process is true for both women and men, but culturally, from a very early age, we label emotional expression as feminine.

I am deeply skeptical about the value, and even the possibility of controlling emotion. Managing emotion is one thing, but controlling it is quite another. G. J. Scrimgeour, in his novel *A Woman of Her Times* had his female character, Elizabeth, say to her son-in-law, "When you feel at your most reasonable, you are acting out of pure emotion, and you cannot tell the difference" (Scrimgeour 1982). Beneath that surface, steely calm of many people, is often a torrent of rage that can erupt in the most destructive manner. This is the "don't get mad, get even" school of response to human emotion. Think, if you will, of Adolf Hitler, Joseph Stalin, and all the dictators who have tortured and maimed millions of their enemies. We consider this behavior to be coldhearted, but perhaps it is actually hothearted, with all the emotions bottled up beneath a cold exterior.

In this chapter I look at how feeling our feelings can actually contribute to our business effectiveness both for the short and long term; how the subjective nature of feeling is also the ground of what I am calling radical trust, by which I mean trust in individual capacity; and how feeling as interpreted by Jungian depth psychology is a powerful psychic function that can play a major positive role in public life.

SWEET SORROW

The relationship between feeling our feelings and long-term business effectiveness was made clear to me in an unusual way. In the midst of a business crisis, my husband and partner, Bob, had a dream in which he was walking with a little old lady whom he adored, experiencing delight in her company. Then she got into a sailboat and sailed away, leaving him smitten with tremendous sorrow and loss. In the dream he found himself walking around in tears, feeling very proud of his pathos, really savoring the sweetness of that sorrow.

In real life when he runs with our local volunteer ambulance, he experiences this sweet sorrow over and over again. Most of the patients out here in the country are old. Many are facing death, if not today, one day soon. His job is to get them to the hospital in stable condition so that the medical personnel can try to save them. As painful as this work is, I have watched him reap enormous benefits from being really present with someone in a moment of immense physical stress. This is truly one of the sweetest and most mysterious moments in life.

The dream, his dream coach Clare Keller suggested, offered him the insight that he was not allowing himself to feel the same sweet sorrow when hit by an unexpected business loss. This was enormously helpful information for both of us. In difficult times, my friends will often tell me to "trust the universe." I would like to believe that trusting the universe means that something good will happen before I crash and burn, that is, that a new piece of business will appear out of the blue to replace the one I have just lost. But the phoenix rising from the ashes is the more accurate version of what is likely to happen. In other words, replacing business, particularly when the existing form of business has become dysfunctional, takes time. New business rarely just "shows up"; it needs to be painstakingly built. Chances are I will have to experience my old business in ashes, including the financial base on which I have been counting, before the new business will emerge.

The faith that I need to have, then, is more like the willingness to experience the sorrow of the loss, the willingness to sink into it so I can know its sweetness, as I would want to experience the sweet sorrow that comes with the loss of a loved one. Without feeling grief for a lost loved one, there is no way to go on with one's life as a whole human being. If I cannot let myself feel the same thing in my business, right down to my bones, I cannot get to the place where I can see what other options I have—not just the safe options, but the options for real creativity. I am too preoccupied with struggling to resuscitate my old business, hanging onto the security it gave me and warding off what looks to me like a defeat.

As businesspeople we face upheavals in our work lives almost every day. Entropy, or the natural deterioration of physical matter—and I would add the natural deterioration of systems, communications, timetables, and just about everything we can plan for—is the normal state of affairs. In a business group that I belonged to, one member, a builder, said he was struggling with bringing his projects in on time and within budget estimates. His colleague, also a builder, who had national experience and a wide reputation for his integrity, told him he was asking the wrong question. The project will always be late, he continued, and it will always be over budget. The real question to struggle with is how to manage that reality.

When we're under perpetual stress, we have no time to go deep, to sink into the sorrow produced by the really major upsets in our work lives. It is hard enough to face up to a loss when it comes as the result of natural entropy on a small scale in a particular business. What, then, when the problem is the result of a basic shift in economic reality, when many businesses are affected by a change so basic that we have to let go of our previous assumptions and structures and start over on the long and uncertain path of building something new? This kind of basic change is easiest to see when there is a major breakthrough in technology. The automobile, and then air travel, for example, drastically altered the economies of railroads and railroad workers in particular, and mainframe computer businesses will never be the same because of the emergence of PCs.

But the shift away from heavy manufacturing as a whole and toward information-based economies is more subtle and actually more massive. Although the information-based future looks bright, we are a long way from feeling the full brunt of social disruption as we let go of our heavily consumption-based industrial economy and correct its environmental excesses. This is well illustrated by the short euphoria that followed President Clinton's election in 1992. For some people there was a feeling that we might actually get a grip on our national problems. This feeling was reminiscent of the excitement that we felt at President Kennedy's inauguration when he called on a whole generation to "ask not what your country can do for you; ask what you can do for your country." But what national will had mounted in the few weeks after Clinton's inauguration broke down quickly when details emerged of various proposals for addressing our national debt, health care, and environmental issues. Immediately all kinds of groups began to lobby against those aspects of the proposals that would have the greatest economic impact on their constituencies.

This behavior is a normal part of the political process in a democracy, but the extent of our unwillingness to suffer any setbacks was very telling. The political stalemate that we are currently experiencing goes beyond partisan politics, because it seems that no matter which party puts forth a proposal, the opposition is less based on principle than on the desire to avoid loss. This stalemate, it seems to me, is a result of a failure to recognize and accept at a deep enough level the enormity of change that is before us. To feel the sorrow of these potential losses to our bones is what it may take before we can collectively see around the bend to a future that might be far better than what we can currently imagine.

We have so little space to feel at this level in our public life in general, and in business in particular, that it has occurred to me that we could use a transition house, a place like a drug rehabilitation center, where we could give over the struggle to hold everything together to someone else and dry out. I've imagined turning my house into such a center, cooking for the participants and encouraging them to walk around the pond and through the garden, to sing and read stories aloud at night. We could call this Businesspeople's Anonymous, a twelve-step program for all of us who are adrift in this economic system, not yet able to see or to admit that it is totally beyond our control. Maybe together we could muster the courage to experience the great sweet sorrow of the industrial age so we can let it go.

Women are generally less determined to control their emotions than men are, at least in part because women have had a far less rigid education in that department. If my belief is accurate that there are some rocky times ahead for our economic system, then women's ability to express emotions can be of enormous help with the transitions we will have to make. I have an image in my mind of a beautiful woman in a workshop I attended. She was facing the loss of a brother to cancer at any moment. The intensity of her grief—her willingness to share it and her acceptance of it in herself—was the centerpiece of the work that we did that weekend. It helped everyone else come to terms with whatever feelings they were struggling to accept. That woman demonstrated to all of us that getting real feelings on the table can help others to do the same. If we can do that in business, we can increase our chances of moving beyond our emotions to fundamentally new considerations.

OMAHA BEACH AND RADICAL TRUST

The reality of the pain that exists in the world, especially in times of change, was very present to me during the fiftieth anniversary of D day. The special programming caught me by surprise. I was hooked after seeing one documentary that spliced together old newsreel footage with interviews of surviving veterans. Who were these men who had become so articulate, so vulnerable as a result of having performed so heroically? Their lives became important to me as I struggled to understand what they had experienced and how it had changed them. I felt enormous pain about the loss of their comrades, whose lives were so expendable in the midst of combat yet so precious to someone back home.

One of life's paradoxes is that the sacredness of individual lives does not spare them from sacrifice. It must have been a bittersweet moment for Eisenhower when he visited the paratroopers before the invasion: he knew most of them would not return. As we change our economic and political systems in our own time, many of us will be casualties. I am already aware of the anguish of people laid off after years of service, and of people who, because of some spiritual calling, can no longer do what they have always done but who still have a mortgage to pay and a family to feed. The physical disruption is very real.

But there were other lessons from D day besides pain. I was deeply moved by what the Allied troops managed to do on that day, especially on Omaha Beach, and I wanted to know what their experience could tell me about the effort needed in my own time. Because it sometimes feels to me like I am up against my own Omaha Beach in terms of figuring out what I need to do, or what I *can* do to contribute to our planetary survival and well-being.

At Omaha Beach, the American troops expected to encounter their toughest resistance *after* they had taken the fortified bluffs overlooking the beach. Instead they found themselves pinned down on the beach by enemy fire, in total chaos, the "plan" gone awry. As each man told of his experience there, he said something like this: "This was not about the officers, you know. They were gone. One by one, two by two, the private soldiers had to decide what to do."

Hitler, said historian Stephen Ambrose, was contemptuous of the invasion. He thought American "boy scouts" could never stand up to the discipline of the German totalitarian state. At that point in history, people really wondered which would emerge the postwar victor: totalitarianism or communism. Democracy was, in many minds, not even in the running (Moyers 1994).

But on Omaha Beach, those American boy scouts found a way to move inland from the beach despite murderous enemy fire. And in some cases the Allies were aided by the fact that German officers were waiting for orders before reacting to the situation in front of them. Both historian Ambrose and the soldiers who were there agree: it was the individual initiative of leaderless American GIs, the result of years of American civic training, that made it possible for so many young men, most never having seen combat before, to take the situation into their own hands and get off the beach.

I could see from what happened at Omaha Beach how likely it is that the best of plans will break down under stress. When the breakdown happened there, a paradoxical thing occurred. The bond between the soldiers, their esprit de corps, deepened, making the effort bearable. At the same time, the normal patterns of leadership were broken; each soldier had to rely on his own inner authority, his own inner ability to assess reality and respond.

This effort is an example of radical trust, radical trust in individual capacity—one's own and that of others—in a background of deep community. Because of this support, individuals can often gain the strength needed to give the best they can personally give. Although women have rarely played a major role in war, individual strength within community is familiar territory for them. Women may not consider themselves risktakers in the usual heroic fashion, but the capacity and experience of giving birth to a new being through their bodies makes them uniquely capable of seeing the inherent, subjective value of each person. Being a parent requires radical trust. Once a child is born, the job of the father and the mother is to get that unique being into the best possible shape for the inevitable moment of leaving the nest.

This radical trust in individuals is what is so often missing today in groups, business and otherwise, who are trying to find a new way. Organizationally we forget to rely on our troops, and we forget to train our troops to adopt an attitude and capacity to trust themselves in the moment. We also get caught up in elitism, based on notions of quality or capacity that we have developed through our current belief systems and life experience. We think we already know what skills will be needed in the future and who will be the critical players. But making major changes in our business systems may require more diverse manifestations of human capacity than we are now capable of recognizing institutionally. Ironically another lesson from wartime is that we need to accept everyone who is willing to participate. When there is a draft, you have to prove yourself incapable of serving rather than the other way around.

THE SUBJECTIVE GROUND OF DEEP FEELING AND RADICAL TRUST

A major connection between allowing yourself to feel deeply and having radical trust in people is a respect for subjectivity. We understand completely what it means to see the world objectively. We are accustomed to looking for observable and verifiable information outside ourselves. Subjectivity has to do with experiencing what is going on *within* ourselves—what we feel, what we believe, what is the nature of our being.

Both objective and subjective realities are valid, but we live in a world that is obsessed with objectivity, as if it were the only truth. Most journalists, for example, seem unaware that the objectivity with which they proudly credit themselves is a subjective point of view, because, in their inner frame of reference, objectivity is all there is. This one-sidedness is a major blind spot in our media-driven culture. Reporters are expected to be skeptical about everything. To be otherwise is to be considered naive. As soon as a reporter subjectively experiences the emotion or insights of the participants of an event—which is not the same thing as reporting on other people's emotional responses as a "human interest" angle of a story—that reporter is no longer considered capable of delivering an unbiased report.

But how can someone actually report the whole truth without having the experience? Loving and caring are good examples of experiences you can have only if you are willing to be the subject. Sexuality is certainly another. So is spirituality. You can write a good, objective story about a successful marriage or even a business, but the only way to *have* a good marriage or a thriving business is to live it, to be inside of it, which is a highly subjective experience.

I am so convinced about the importance of this subjective experience for the future not only of busiess but for the whole human species that I am more interested in watching the subjective reality of each individual emerge than I am in just about anything else. I am obsessed with authenticity. I believe intuitively that only if we develop our individual nature can we do our best work. Good skills will not be enough. I also believe that as the human species evolves, something new is being asked of all of our systems, especially business, something that may not have been needed, or at least not to the same extent, in the past. Everywhere I look organizations are in turmoil. What seems to have worked before is no longer working. The word "dysfunctional" is increasingly applied to our families, organizations, and communications, although I doubt they are functioning much differently from what appeared to be normal and successful several decades ago. In business organizations I have worked in, normally competent, compassionate people seem to be rising to a new level of incompetence en masse, almost in direct proportion to their positive intentions.

We seem to be newly aware that something else is possible. But what we are seeing is *not* about collective action as we have viewed it in the past, just as the collective work of women that I described in the last chapter is not the same as "the collective" in communist states. The new vision is about the meshing of many authentic natures, each one subjective, such that a greater productivity occurs without either an externally determined hierarchy or mass conformity. Now try to hold that idea in your mind rather than jumping to your favorite theories about organizations. This is one of those areas where our greatest obstacle might be assuming that we already "know" something.

Recently I stood outside in the sunshine at an airport after coming back from a tumultuous meeting of a nonprofit business organization. I thought for the billionth time that, if only the group could get its *thinking* clear, the conflicts would resolve themselves, and we would be able to move ahead in sync, like the drops of water in a wave. But maybe the new form of organization we are trying to learn requires something other than clear thinking. Maybe the key opportunity is to struggle messily with our relationships, that is, putting our feelings and concerns on the table without initially knowing how to resolve the conflicts that arise between us.

This kind of struggle requires radical trust in human beings. It also involves radical trust that we will eventually be successful in working out our problems. The revolutionary action of our time, it seems to me, is to tolerate the chaos until a new organizational form emerges. This seems parallel to the experience of the Founding Fathers in the late 1700s. What many of the makers of the Constitution trusted radically were the principles of the Age of Reason. They believed that each individual person had an innate access to reason, and reason, to them, was more than logic. It had a quality of divine inspiration about it; it was a capacity within human beings to understand the nature of reality and respond appropriately. From this basic belief in people, the designers of the Constitution developed an experiment in democracy that gave more power to more people than anywhere in the Western world, and few believed it could work. Our forefathers had an uncanny understanding that the form of government—that is, the way we collectively relate to each other—was the substance of the revolution itself, not just the vehicle.

I believe that the way we collectively relate to each other is also the substance of our current revolution, and that the feminine principle has much to contribute to this effort to evolve to an even higher, more participatory form of organization—in our homes, our businesses, and in our government. Enduring the chaos—staying with feelings in the here and now—and using diffuse awareness to pick up and sort data that at first glance does not seem to be relevant, will be as least as important, in my mind, as coming up with a brilliant idea.

FEELING AS VALUE

Furthermore, when we think of deep feeling and radical trust in people, it is helpful to understand "feeling" as the Jungians did—as an active psychic function, not just as emotion. Just as scientists have broken down substances of the earth into elements, Jung broke down the psyche into these four functions: sensation, intuition, thinking, and feeling. Sensation and intuition, he suggested, are the functions we use to take in information. Thinking and feeling are functions we use to make judgments and decisions.

I find it interesting that Jung associated feeling, as well as thinking, with judgment. "Feeling" is used here as a verb and is not the same as experiencing feelings (noun). The same is true for thinking. Active thinking, in Jung's mind, was different from being passively aware of thoughts. Thinking, he said, involved "the linking up of ideas by means of a concept" (Jung 1971, 481). One example would be Newton's observations of apples uniformly dropping from trees and his development of the concept of gravity. Each time I watch an apple drop, I *think* of the concept of gravity and make the judgment that this is one way that the universe works. My judgment is about the accuracy of the concept: such and such is an accurate description of what happens in such and such a condition, or it is not.

Feeling, on the other hand, involves giving value to what you are thinking about. It involves judgment of a very different order, an evaluation of right or wrong, goodness or badness. We are feeling when we accept or reject something, when we like or dislike something, or when we feel appreciation or disapproval. Putting together information to decide whether or not a certain ethnic group is being discriminated against has to do with thinking; not liking the fact that they are being discriminated against has to do with feeling. Feeling is by nature subjective because it originates from values within. When we are feeling intensely, that function may well be accompanied by affect, that is, by feeling in the body, thus our association of feeling with emotion.

What does it mean to make decisions on the basis of feeling? Since I am a person with a strong tendency toward my feeling function, I can give you a personal example. I used to have vanity license plates that read NO WAR, which were given to me by my sister-in-law during my years of working with the Beyond

War movement. For several years those plates were so much a part of me that I often forgot they were there until some gas station attendant would come to the window smiling and say how much he liked my plates. I would feel a shock of pleasure and surprise that he noticed and that he agreed enough with my views to mention it. It was exhilarating to feel that so many people were actually understanding and supporting the message that was at the heart of Beyond War: we can no longer afford to fight wars without taking the risk of destroying the whole earth system with nuclear arms.

As the Gulf War approached, however, my reality shifted. One December night when my husband and I were driving home, some drunk young men in a car observed the plates and then screamed obscenities at us and tailgated us dangerously. On some days I would drive down the street and notice people giving me the high sign, and I knew by the hostility behind their gestures that they saw my message as strictly a political opposition to President Bush. Then one day I was told about a woman I had met in my town who had two sons in the service, both of whom had been shipped to the Gulf. What a nasty shock and surprise that must have been for her, I thought, in this time when so many young people enter the service as a way to get an education and start a career.

When the war broke out in January, I had a long talk with myself. I was truly afraid of being driven off the road and increasingly hesitated before going out at night. But I was also chagrined that I might be a coward if I let that feeling drive my behavior. What a row there was going on in my head! Slowly it dawned on me that the circumstances had changed the meaning of the message. The plates were now provoking hostility, which was not at all what I meant to do.

While working in Beyond War, I had studied the principle of capitulation, which meant that we should yield to reality instead of trying to force another outcome. Since the Beyond War goal was to "be one," that is, to be in relationship with everyone on a planet that could no longer afford war as a way of resolving conflict, we did not press our point on someone who was not ready to hear it. Now I had the opportunity, in real life, to understand what capitulation meant. I had to capitulate to the reality that we were not yet Beyond War, capitulate to the feelings of people who were suffering from the war far more than I was, and capitulate to the realization that I was naive to think that a license plate could convey a complex thought in a time of such political tension. I finally removed the plates, though I had to go through a lot of personal feeling first. It was a lot more than license plates that were at stake; my identity was on the line too.

My Beyond War experience helped me to find the principle upon which I could justify a decision, the basic direction of which had been initiated by a feeling I had about what was the right thing for me to do. I was grateful for the extraordinary work Beyond War had done in formulating what we called, "a new way of thinking," but I knew what I wanted to do before I had thought it through. The real reason I removed my NO WAR license plates was that I could not bear to think of that woman in my town with two sons in the Gulf seeing my plates and feeling hurt by my apparent indifference to her fear for her sons. It was just not right for me to do that to another person. I had not changed my thinking about war at all; in fact, I felt tremendous disappointment that we resorted to military action instead of making a real attempt to resolve the conflict with economic measures. But I made my judgment about the plates using my feeling function, and I would have done so even had it ultimately been in contradiction with my thinking function.

The fact that I had to link my decision to the principle of capitulation before I could be at ease with it in my own mind illustrates how much clearer we are in our culture about the thinking function than we are about the feeling function. We say "I think" almost all the time, when some of the time we really mean "I feel." We say, "I feel bad about X," meaning I have feelings about the situation. But we very rarely say, "I *feel* this is the wrong decision." Instead we say, "I *think* this is the wrong decision." When we actually *do* say that we don't feel right about a decision, we are often discounted or patronized. We even do it to ourselves.

This phenomenon is all the more present in business situations. I will often find myself resisting an action suggested by colleagues or clients. I cannot say that I always disagree with their assessment of a situation or their conclusions about what needs to be done. But I resist, nonetheless, while chastising myself for being unclear, weak, and indecisive. When I examine my resistance, I see that I am most often concerned about offending someone or pushing someone inappropriately. I am thinking about the whole situation, all the repercussions on people. Until I have sorted out all the details in my mind and decided what I *feel* is right, I cannot go forward effectively. Now some of this struggle is surely rooted in personal issues, but not all of it. Jung says that the feeling function makes a valuation of the *whole* conscious situation. In my experience that is very true. Evaluating the whole conscious situation would be the natural thing to do, if I am perceiving what is happening in a diffuse way.

When my feeling comes into play, it certainly slows me down. I do not believe that feeling operates inherently more slowly than thinking, because resistance in my body comes into play almost immediately. But the current business culture gives so little credence to the feeling function that my first reaction to a strong feeling is hesitation, even paralysis, until I can come up with a good reason to justify what I feel. Over time, I have come to trust both functions more evenly. When I engage my thinking function in a business situation, I get a better understanding of what is objectively true in the external environment, and I can see which of my concerns are unfounded. When I engage my feeling function and take the time to sort out why I feel the way I do, I very often make a decision that solves the problem while preserving and, I hope, even enhancing existing relationships.

Once again, relationship is a critical concept. We need both good thinking, which gives us an accurate, conceptual picture of what is real, and good feeling, which gives us our deep sense of relatedness to the world in which we live. Gaining practice and mastery in the feeling function is our best hope for consciously, and on a daily basis, including the health of our planet in our decisions about the use of resources and processes of production. Such mastery will also enhance our human relationships and *real* quality of life. Women have an important contribution to make in bringing the feeling function into play in the workplace. Katherine Briggs and Isabel Briggs Myers developed the Myers-Briggs Type Indicator (MBTI) expressly to measure individual preferences such as thinking and feeling. It will not come as a surprise that on the thinking-feeling continuum, the percentage of women who prefer the feeling function over the thinking function ranges from the mid-fifties to the mid-sixties (McCaulley 1994, 16). Although we all use both functions, having a "preference" for one or the other is similar to being right-handed or left-handed. Imagine what a handicap it would be if you had to lead with your left hand when you are clearly right-handed. Really imagine what it would be like for you, if every day you had to work with your weakest hand, maybe even with your strongest hand tied behind your back. For businesspeople with a preference for the feeling function, every day requires this kind of accommodation.

The MBTI statistics show us two seemingly contradictory things. More women than men have a preference for their feeling function, yet there *are* men who prefer their feeling function—in the range of 15 to 25 percent. One wonders whether this percentage of men would be higher were there not so much cultural pressure on men to develop their thinking function. The MBTI statistics tell us that we are *all* capable of understanding and using the strengths of both thinking and feeling, which means that there is plenty of room for collaboration.

Nonetheless, when I have worked in traditional business settings with men who are conscious of having a feeling preference, most of these men have looked to women for leadership in this area. I have been curious about this phenomenon for a long time and have finally come to the conclusion that there is something in the pecking order that men learn from a very early age that makes it very difficult for them to bring real feeling into corporate structures. As adrift as I myself have felt in my efforts to bring the feeling function into conscious play in certain business situations, I have not felt the same kind of disorientation that I sense these men have felt. It seems to me, therefore, that without the leadership of women it is unlikely that we will fine-tune our understanding and mastery of feeling so that it can be put to good business use.

As we undergo unprecedented changes, the conscious expression of deep feeling—both by revealing the pain that we experience in our work lives and by articulating our deepest values—can make an enormous difference for the future of business. So, too, can the ability to radically trust individual capacity. A model for such expression of feeling and trust can be found in an area of human activity that we rarely associate with business. In the next chapter we will consider what it means to mother and to be mothered, and how these functions, seen in a new light, can contribute to public life.

Chapter 8

Mothering and Being Mothered

I'm talking here about a deep father figure that settles into the soul to provide a sense of authority, the feeling that you are the author of your own life, that you are the head of the household in your own affairs.

All mothering, whether in a family or within an individual, is made up of both affectionate caring and bitter emotional pain. . . . In both emotions, the mother is close to the child, allowing the child, even as she feels pain and anger, to become an individual through exposure to experience and to fate.

—THOMAS MOORE, *Care of the Soul*

As I watched a high school soccer play-off game, I overheard a spectator say to a mother that her star athlete daughter always seemed to "carry the whole world on her shoulders." And, indeed, this player played her game with grim determination and intense seriousness. Her mother replied, "Yes, but that is just her nature. It is not good to bark at her."

As I watched the fierce play on the field, I thought hard about that comment. For surely the daughter had plenty of fathering, if Moore's statement is right that fathering provides a sense of one's own authority. In terms of her mastery of the game on the field, there was no question that this player was the author of her own life. Yet her mother saw another angle; the girl had to author her life in accordance with her own nature. It is useful to look at the mother's comment again. She did *not* say, "It *does no good* to bark at her." She said, "It is not *good* to bark at her."

This chapter looks at mothering as that human activity that nurtures and defends the essential and unique nature of human beings. The soccer player's mother understood that not only would it be impossible to change the girl's nature, but it would be inappropriate. The "affectionate caring" of motherhood and its "bitter emotional pain" are inextricably linked by the very closeness the mother feels to the child. This closeness paradoxically gives the child space to be fully known, because the mother is interested in everything about the child. It also motivates the mother to support the child's essence at all emotional costs. Ultimately the mother both lets go and holds on. The mother lets go of the child to allow the child to face his or her own experience and fate, but she never lets go of her love attachment to the child, thus the "bitter emotional pain."

THE CHARGE ASSOCIATED WITH "MOTHER"

I have experienced a lot more good fathering in the business world than good mothering. I can think of any number of male mentors who have helped me understand and gain confidence in my own business skills—accountants, sales reps, lawyers, and managers. All of them have communicated to me in one way or another that I could do something and have offered me specific coaching. Good fathering, as Moore suggests, helps people find their own sense of authority, in other words, their ability to act effectively in the world (Moore 1994). We may have varying opinions about what good fathering is, but we rarely question its value in the public sphere, because it helps us acquire the skills that we need to succeed.

Mothering, on the other hand, is something that we don't think of as belonging in business. All the actual mothers in business are preoccupied with not appearing to be mothers, and *everyone* is preoccupied with not appearing to need mothering. The very use of the word "mothering" in a chapter heading for this book made many people uncomfortable. There was a strong desire to convert "mothering" to something more generic, like "nurturing"; but, as you will see later in this chapter, nurturing does not cover all the possible forms of mothering.

Why are the words "mother" and "mothering" so charged not only in public life but in adult life in general? I believe this is because, in our world of focused consciousness, everything is seen as being polarized—better or worse, higher or lower, more or less complicated. Mothering is fine for children, but an insult if you are "grown-up." It implies a lack of autonomy, an unhealthy weakness and dependence. Fathering, which can also be seen as mentoring, is far less threatening to our sense of individual competence.

A problem that adds to the discomfort we feel about mothering is that women sometimes assume a false mothering posture that has more to do with their own agenda to be liked or to avoid appearing to be saying no than with real empathy. It can also be a way to establish control and position: a woman in business can convey a sense of superiority when she is mothering someone. This behavior may remind us too much of the times when we have felt smothered by our mother's influence. Too much mothering is suffocating; it is the mother figure holding on to fill some inner need and not letting the child have his or her own experience and fate. Similarly too much fathering can be controlling; it does not foster the growth of the child's authority but imposes its own authority instead.

My experience with a female bank loan officer who once called me about a loan application illustrates this false mothering. She asked me a lot of questions about my business and responded enthusiastically to what I told her, almost too uniformly, and then turned me down, still all bubbly and sweet. Since she only knew me through that telephone call, and since

she clearly had no intention of taking a risk on me, her efferves-
cence sounded patronizing and inauthentic.

POSITIVE MOTHERING IN BUSINESS

Mothering as a human activity may be "natural," but it is not
automatically well done. To increase workers' authentic appreciation of themselves and to enhance their performance, it
takes conscious effort and a genuine and *specific* enjoyment of
people—not a facade of enjoyment that fits conventional pre-
scriptions about how women should feel and behave. Women
who are mothers understand just how intense and difficult it can
be to love a child totally. Loving so totally draws out of them the
capacity to affirm the child's nature, even if they suspect that
nature will someday break their heart. This attention to individual nature is just as important to ongoing adult growth as is
the fathering that helps us become the authors of our own lives,
and it is not possible to give someone this kind of individual
attention without being attached to him or her.

Being a small business owner, I have experienced a lot more
freedom to become personally attached to my employees than I
imagine would have been possible in some larger businesses. On
the rare occasion when I specified objectively what I wanted in a
new employee, I ended up reversing myself 180 degrees, because
the person who showed up for the interview was so terrific that
I decided I wanted what she had to offer instead. Since I was not
restricted by my original perception of what I wanted, the person
who presented herself opened me up to opportunities I had not
foreseen. Earlier, I had actually offered a position to a person on
the objective basis of my job description and had been relieved
when she turned me down. These quirks in my hiring process
never resulted in bad decisions for the company as far as I
could see.

I also noticed that employees stayed with us. Despite the
stories they could probably tell about our inadequacies and in-
consistencies as employers, nobody was in a hurry to leave. In

fact, my staff was actually concerned that the employee for whom I reversed myself 180 degrees would last only a matter of months because she was overqualified. Three years later this woman left reluctantly because I did not have the business to keep her. This was my first layoff, and I was heartbroken.

I really liked the people I hired. I loved their successes and suffered over their discomfort and failures. I loved their innovations, not only for what they offered the company, but also because I enjoyed watching them unfold. I believe we mother and are mothered by each other constantly throughout life. The same is true for fathering and being fathered. This is a constant in human relatedness that we cannot get away from, and I don't expect it to be absent from my work life.

I also loved how my staff mothered me. I remember well the day when I told my new business manager that I was concerned about getting a large receivable in time to make payroll. I had worked for weeks to set up the payment schedule so the check would arrive in time. I told her in jest, but with a grain of truth beneath it, that if the check didn't get to us in time, I would probably want to throw myself under a truck. She replied, in a totally matter-of-fact tone, "Well, we'll want to keep an eye on you then, won't we?"

Mothering, then, involves both the tendency to keep others out of harm's way and, at its essence, valuing human beings for their own sake and communicating that care. I have a friend, Linda Atkins, in Maine, who is a master at telling people, in the most genuine way, what is good about them and their work. I notice that I never miss a chance to call her to share my successes as well as my failures.

Mothering involves affirming individual worth, that value and combination of talents within us that is uniquely ours; fathering is equally important in affirming our accomplishments and potential for acquiring new skills. We could all use far more than we get of the mirroring of our nature that good mothering offers, and we could all give it to others far more than we do. When it comes to business leadership, providing good training and maintaining order are essential. But neither the best order nor the best training, alone, is likely to produce dynamic creativity in situations we cannot plan for. Only strong individual self-esteem can do that. And as the principal of a leading-edge interim management firm observed, self-esteem takes on a new importance in an economy that is becoming increasingly knowledge dependent. Business leaders need to create high comfort levels for employees in knowledge-based companies in order for the employees to give their best. If workers don't trust themselves, nor their company's willingness as an employer to hear *all* of what they have learned, the company may not get the full data it needs to remain competitive.

Since mothering involves experiencing the inherent worth of others, it is no wonder that we can feel such bitter emotional pain when we have to allow others to be exposed to their individual experience and fate. This is the downside of mothering in business as in other aspects of life. Failure to carry through on this aspect of the role is what gives mothering a reputation for being suffocating rather than supportive of personal growth. Keeping people out of harm's way is important but not, by itself, enough. Having the radical trust to allow people to have their own experience and fate is essential.

In some cases good mothering actually involves kicking a fledgling out of the nest when the fledgling has stayed too long. Employees and managers are constantly facing the challenge of allowing their people to have their own experience and fate. I am not talking about massive layoffs that are impersonal, although our current economic difficulties have certainly increased the frequency with which we are having to acknowledge that we cannot protect people from individual pain and loss. Good mothering in these and other situations means staying connected to the other person while not trying to assume the fate that legitimately belongs to another.

I have coached enough people out of my company to know how painful the process is. One employee became increasingly dissatisfied with his work as the focus of our company shifted from advertising and marketing. He wanted the company to design work for him according to the old model that he liked. He did not understand that we were struggling as hard as we could to develop alternatives in a changing marketplace. I could not protect him from the changes to which he could not adjust, and eventually we worked out a plan. He stayed on with us for a month at full salary, using his time and the resources of the office to find other work. When the day came for him to leave, I struggled with my guilt, but it was neither possible nor appropriate for me to try to find meaningful work for him. He needed to create his own work by interacting with the marketplace.

In another instance I did not act soon enough. A young woman in my employ was restless for a different kind of challenge than I could offer her. We discussed it briefly and thought about designing a plan to help her explore what other work might be available while she continued her work at our company. But we both got distracted and busy, so that four months later a downturn in business necessitated a hasty and painful layoff. I walked into her room after the decision was made, and we put our arms around each other and cried. It was unavoidable, but it was also awful, and I felt responsible for not having foreseen what would happen. I do not think it is inappropriate to feel for the people I work with or to hope that others will care for me similarly. As painful as this situation was, it was better than what happened to a female manager I spoke with. She had been laid off by a boss who barely talked with her or looked her in the eyes for the two weeks before he laid her off. When he finally told her, she felt like he was reading a script. "I don't lay people off that way," she said. "I meet their eyes. Sometimes I even hug them."

THE MOTHER BEAR SYNDROME: FEMININE RAGE

There is another aspect of mothering, one of enormous ferocity, which we all equate with the behavior of the mother bear. I would never have thought of this capacity in regard to mothering in business if I had not had the following experience. I was at a board meeting of a business organization, one of those rushed sessions where we could have used five times the amount of time we had. People had come from many cities, too, so the time got cut even shorter because people had to get back to the airport to catch flights home. We were trying to complete an assessment of a strategic plan and still have time left over to finish a previous conversation about a report on the status of our membership, a report about which I had a lot of concern.

In the middle of our assessment someone interjected an extraneous, negative comment about the membership report. One of the report's opponents capitalized on the remark with a joke, but there the conversation ended because we had to press on with the business at hand.

For me something had changed in the room. I sensed a deliberate poisoning of the atmosphere, and it was aimed at the membership report. I realized that we would probably not have time to clear it up. There was so much feeling in me about this negative comment that I had to work hard to stay present to the strategic plan. At the time I could formulate no plan of action that would have satisfied me. When I think back on this, I wish I had insisted on further discussion about the membership report regardless of the time issue. To have spoken up would not have been very savvy, but I wish I had done it anyway.

Like the mother bear, my concern was for the young. In this case I was worried about the ordinary members of the organization who were trying to be heard about how their needs were not being met. I can still feel the rage in me at what I perceived to be a manipulative effort to thwart the membership's communication with the board by discrediting the report.

In business, women as well as men have learned to be smart—we have learned to keep our mouths shut until we know the most effective thing to say, to plan out strategic action that will result in a win. The mother bear follows a different strategy; she will simply tear you to pieces if you get between her and her offspring. She doesn't care if she has any power base when she is done. It doesn't matter who lines up on her side. You are simply done for if you threaten her babes.

I wonder what the effect would have been if I had followed my instincts to go for the throat during the board meeting. I am very rarely provoked to this kind of behavior; such an intense response has to come from deep inside, and it is *always* associated with the perception that some individual or group is in imminent danger—comparable to one's offspring facing the strength and superior intelligence of some much larger creature that would make the weaker creature its prey.

There is only one time that I can remember actually doing this in a business context. We were producing a television commercial, and as usual, it was a very long day. We had started at 4 A.M., as I recall. We had five major scenes to film, some involving the participation of the client's employees, many of whom had arrived late for their scenes. When you're filming a commercial, even when everyone arrives like clockwork on the set, there are always unforeseen complications—a difficult corner to light, champagne that won't bubble at just the right moment, an actor who has difficulty remembering his lines. As a result of such difficulties we were at least three hours behind schedule. It was 8 P.M., dinner had arrived for my hungry and exhausted crew, and I wanted to set it up in a certain location. The client came in and objected, wanting to shuttle us off to the basement, which would be much less comfortable. I was furious. I could not change his mind, but I did not hide how I felt. These were my people, and they deserved better treatment.

Now this client was a very powerful man; people rarely crossed him without suffering dire repercussions. I could see my office manager's face go white with fear as she witnessed our encounter, but I did not budge. Later the same client, who was also a personal friend, came down to the basement. He wrapped his arms around me as if we were wrestling and said, "Come on, hit me." I got both messages he was sending: that he understood my rage and that he wanted to make up.

At no point in that encounter did I consider backing off from what I felt in order to accommodate him. I was deeply centered and utterly fearless. What I learned from this experience is that if the feeling is real and grounded, even the most powerful opponent may be thrown off the mark, and you may produce the result you want without getting damaged. I did not win the immediate battle at hand, but I did not lose the client either.

There have been so many other times in similar business situations when I have either become hysterical or simply lost my nerve and faded into the woodwork. What made this occasion different? When I look back on it I can see that the response came from my body not my mind. It was so truly instinctive, and so much in defense of something beyond myself, that I did not think to question it. Nor was I attached to a particular outcome. I never had the thought that I had failed because I did not succeed in convincing my client to change his mind. The rightness of the response was inherent in itself, unassociated with any particular idea of what it meant to win or lose. Perhaps this is why I could not be thrown off my course. This experience reinforces my belief that the real revolutionary action of our time is going deep within ourselves and discovering what we are capable of rather than trying to make external changes in our personalities or in our environment based on what we currently know.

I am trying to imagine what results we might see in business if we became confident enough to allow this instinctive response to come forth full force—not only in defense of other people, but in defense of the water supply, the air, and the earth. I am not suggesting indiscriminate rage here, but something primal whose very rarity would make everyone sit up and take notice. Each person would have to know himself or herself well and be able to differentiate this instinct from a more generalized anger, or ego-based rage, or oversensitivity.

How does one know when rage is primal and when it is ego-based? The difference may not be as difficult to distinguish as one might think. Like diffuse awareness, our primal feminine rage may be something we have not thought about enough to make it conscious in our minds, but we may recognize it instinctively when we experience it. The endless amount of material written about the masculine heroic experience is a good place to look for a model of how we could observe, and then articulate, what happens in the feminine process. Just as the feminine is capable of a mother bear response to life that transcends ego, the masculine is also capable of knowing when protecting one's turf is essential and worth dying for and when violent action is based simply on the ego's desire for power.

Reading good war novels, such as W. E. B. Griffin's series about military life, has provided me with a good picture of how men know intuitively when another man is acting from ego and when he is acting from an inner strength that is operating in service to something larger than himself. Griffin is notorious for ridiculing officers who are self-important, and who abuse their rank to damage others below them in the hierarchy. His *real* heroes are noted for two traits. First they use all of their considerable capacity to discern what is really happening in the situations in which they find themselves, whether it is combat, intelligence operations, or logistics. Then they develop and implement a strategy to accomplish their mission with a minimum loss of life. Secondly, the older, more experienced men use their rank to give special opportunities to gifted younger men, as well as to correct whatever injustices have occurred as a result of a power-based system, that is, a system in which an egocentric lieutenant, a commissioned officer, can make life miserable for a noncommissioned corporal or anyone else below him in rank. The *good* soldiers are not without their ego concerns and petty moments, but their peers and subordinates know these men can be trusted to set ego aside in order to execute a mission competently and fairly.

Although these novels may be romantic in the sense that the good guys, by and large, always make it through dangerous encounters without being killed—and there is always an older, wiser man available to support every young man in trouble—Griffin's enormous command of the details of military life makes the novels very informative. Griffin's work illuminated for me how the masculine system works at its best—even in the midst of its worst manifestations, such as the continuous, energy-draining rivalry between the army and the navy (Griffin 1987–89).

What would be the comparable culture in which the distinction between primal feminine rage and ego-based anger would be illuminated? To answer this question we could use some compelling novels about business in which the heroines know where and when to take a mother bear stand effectively and also have the ability to respond to younger players by coaching them to explore and value their unique nature. Such support for the young would be the feminine equivalent of the generosity of Griffin's heroic officers who taught younger men to recognize their own competence and authority.

Just as the masculine needs to be conscious of its motives for exercising power, so, too, the feminine needs to be conscious of its motives for expressing rage. What am I rising to protect—my position in the pyramid of business or something deeper? Again, the problem for the masculine seems to be to restrain its impulse for action, to let go of the need to assert power. For the feminine, the problem seems to be more one of becoming conscious of the legitimacy of taking action, and bringing it forth, although the same questions about appropriateness are always in the background.

For both the masculine and the feminine the difference between ego-based action and action that supports life has to do with how connected that action is to an understanding of how the world really works. How the world really works in this sense means what is consistent with the laws of nature and the needs of life. Having an accurate picture of reality requires paying close attention as well as having a deep desire to serve. It is that desire to serve that helps us to see what is true for the whole, not just what is true for ourselves. Not only does a commitment to serve

Chapter 9

Sensibility about Space

He believed that people could have no devotion to each other that they did not give at the same time to the place they had in common.

—WENDELL BERRY, *The Memory of Old Jack*

Men often leave the logistics of space to women. This is not always a compliment by any means, but even so, it can be a terrific opportunity. The affinity of the feminine for living in the here and now and experiencing spirit and matter as an integrated whole leads all of us, but women in particular, to pay attention to the relationship between the intangible intention of an activity and the physical space in which it takes place.

More than a "nice touch," I believe that the feminine sensibility about physical space can make a big difference in our collective appreciation of the earth, which, as I suggested earlier will result in an enhanced sense of deep community.

Comfort in physical space is especially important in ou business environments because without it we can feel disco nected from the natural world. As Bob Mang, an entreprene and business consultant who has put his commitment to glo

life increase our chances of seeing reality accurately, but such a commitment also forms the basis for our courage. The courage to be "in harm's way" is another quality of Griffin's heroes, a quality so much a part of their character that it is barely mentioned at all.

As women become more at home in business, I believe, both men and women will not be able to ignore this mother bear phenomenon, which is a feminine pattern of heroism. It seems to be part of the design of life, and I don't think we can expect ourselves to put it aside forever and adapt to exclusively masculine patterns of dealing with conflict and danger. The mix—of masculine and feminine patterns—as it emerges in the future, will be very interesting indeed.

Mothering, then, can be a useful model for understanding how we can nurture and defend the essential and unique nature of human beings, not only in private life but in the public world as well. As individual creativity becomes more critical to our information-based economy, the skills we regard as mothering will become more and more important in the public domain. If we take this one step further, we can see that paying attention to the ability to nurture, protect, and affirm other people's unique natures can apply to place and physical objects as well as to people. In the next chapter, we will look at how the feminine sensibility to physical space can affect the business environment in a positive way.

Chapter 9

Sensibility about Space

He believed that people could have no devotion to each other
that they did not give at the same time to the place they had in
common.

—WENDELL BERRY, *The Memory of Old Jack*

Men often leave the logistics of space to women. This is not
always a compliment by any means, but even so, it can be a
terrific opportunity. The affinity of the feminine for living in the
here and now and experiencing spirit and matter as an integrated whole leads all of us, but women in particular, to pay
attention to the relationship between the intangible intention of
an activity and the physical space in which it takes place.

More than a "nice touch," I believe that the feminine sensibility about physical space can make a big difference in our
collective appreciation of the earth, which, as I suggested earlier,
will result in an enhanced sense of deep community.

Comfort in physical space is especially important in our
business environments because without it we can feel disconnected from the natural world. As Bob Mang, an entrepreneur
and business consultant who has put his commitment to global

sustainability to work with over a decade of community service in the San Francisco Bay Area, has observed,

> Places where people live and work, their surroundings, and even some global ecosystems that all our lives depend on are in decline, largely because of the dominating and pervasive impact of our collective business activity—the very activity on which most of us depend for our livelihoods (Gozdz 1995, 336).

When I moved to Vermont—both my office and my home at the same time—I was surprised to hear the owner of the moving company describing my behavior as repeating a pattern he had seen over and over again. After a short time, he asked me to sit at the door and just direct the movers as to what should go where. Women, he told me, knew exactly how they wanted their homes arranged, and he had decided long ago not to interfere with them when they were "nest building"!

I had not seen this behavior in myself before, nor did I fully understand how important the outside physical environment is to me until I moved to the country. In this chapter I share some of my experiences on the land. I hope I will rekindle your memories of special places and their impact on your life and work.

MOON HOLLOW

One of the great pleasures of country living is getting a daily dose of nature and sharing your enjoyment of all the small familiar things in your environment with those who live in close proximity. On the first truly warm spring day after my second winter here, the sun was shining brightly and the sounds of birds and the smell of the air led me by the nose outdoors. Any excuse, even a trip to the mailbox, was sufficient. At lunch, I took a break and walked down the road to Moon Hollow, the home of my nearest neighbor, Judie Lewis, a half-mile away. I knew for certain that she would be in her garden on such a gorgeous day.

As I walked, the promise of future growth was everywhere. The brook roared; the fields were greener than they had been the day before. New buds were on the trees, and the breeze was warmer even in the shade. As I approached Moon Hollow, I could see Judie leaning over the earth digging up plants on the warm side of the house, a piece of land that is protected by a wall and bathed by the sun, a space that is indisputably hers.

She waved and laughed, not at all surprised that I had come. We share the same low-tech attitude about gardening and particularly about tools—a shovel, a spade, our hands, a bor- rowed rototiller for a tough project, maybe, but no more often than is absolutely necessary. She took a break, and together we sat on the ground amidst her flower beds and picked weeds. She pointed out to me what was growing where in the maze of raised beds that are terraced by planks of wood positioned randomly down the hillside that leads to the brook. A native of North Carolina, Judie has no trouble with Vermont's harsh winters, but she does love the sun. Her face, at fifty-two, can sometimes look twenty-five. She has long light brown hair and she wears flowing clothes that suit her, especially long colorful skirts. In her tank top with her hair pinned up on this particular day, her neck and arms were already brown.

I first saw Judie on the Saturday before Easter in mid-April when we first moved to Vermont three years ago. We were up for the weekend, preparing for the full-scale move of both office and home a few weeks later. She called to invite us to the "boat float," an annual spring ritual. We joined her, her children and their partners, and a number of friends at the brook where, in high rubber boots and carrying sticks or poles, everyone was shepherding small wooden boats through the swirling spring waters. It was not a race; the object was to get down to Moon Hollow without losing your boat, taking as much pleasure in the day as you could along the way. Many boats, I found out later, were veterans that were all the more loved, if the more battered, owing to their longevity.

Moon Hollow is a center of multigenerational social life. Judie lives there with her son, her daughter-in-law, two grand- children, and two Vermont black dogs. Her daughter, a glassblower, lives with her husband nearby. There are chickens, cats, sometimes rabbits, although they were banished for a time after they ate the sprouting broccoli. Most of what happens at Moon Hollow is a spontaneous celebration—mostly of the seasons— and everything that can be done outdoors is done outdoors. We've had early summer bonfires, harvest brunches in the garden, and sledding parties in winter. Parties start when people get there, in the afternoon or the evening, not at a set hour. And there is music—always music, homemade, participatory, and alive. The TV lives upstairs and is never missed.

I took to Judie immediately, but the languid and imprecise pace of country life took some getting used to. I still feel the tension between the contractual and time-sensitive urban/ suburban life that I am connected to by phone and by long-term associations, and the land-based, easy flow of life in my new community. To a New Yorker on the phone, I am hopelessly backwoods; but to many Vermonters, I am still in the fast lane.

Back in the days when I was thinking about making this move, I dreamed one night that a colleague from my teaching days said to me that if I wanted to keep my job in Disneyland, I had better get back in a hurry. Something deep within me knew even then that my Disneyland days were over. I am being de-yuppified up here and reclaiming my place as a creature of the earth.

THE DIFFICULTY IN CREATING GOOD SPACE

Most people cannot make the move that I have made. A lot more wouldn't even if they could. I do not believe it is necessary to live where I do to fine-tune one's sensitivity to the earth. But it *is* difficult, almost anywhere in this society, to build a life without being so surrounded by man-made comforts and security that we fail to experience how life itself works around us. Sometimes I feel as if we are living collectively enshrouded in a gauze of man-made invention. It is hard work just to find places of natural beauty, but it is even more difficult, given our busy schedules, to get *enough* time in the natural world to train our senses to experience nature in the detail and depth we need to feel a part of it.

During my first spring up here, I would walk up the side of my hill to look across to the next ridge. My sister, Arlene, had told me to watch closely for the budding of the trees because there was not just one shade of green but many. I was awestruck by the beauty, but I also had the sense that I was not seeing all of it. My brain was not yet programmed to take it all in, and it still isn't. I had a similar experience one fall weekend in Acadia National Park in Maine. On the first day that I arrived I felt frustrated that I couldn't get connected. Then for three days I left my concerns behind me and immersed myself in the physical world. By the time I left, the colors seemed richer, and the demarcation between land and sky was much more clear. Even the feel of the air on my skin was more pronounced. Some filter in my brain seemed to have gotten unclogged, so that my optical nerves and skin cells were working at full capacity again.

It is not a coincidence that we have this difficulty getting enough exposure to the natural world in our daily lives to be open to truly experiencing all that nature has to offer. We have built and arranged our physical environments to correspond to the tension between mind and body that permeates so many of our various philosophies. Reading Daniel Quinn's *Ishmael* (Quinn 1993) was a milestone for me in understanding my own unconscious persistence in trying to escape from the web of nature. Quinn's eloquent conversation with his gorilla guru turns the world around so that we can see *ourselves* as the caged animals, caged by our own perceptions.

What results from our efforts to escape from the web of nature is a deadening artificiality, a preoccupation with luxuriousness and quantity rather than natural beauty. I suspect, for example, that a constant lack of good natural space—really, a total failure even to understand what that could be—contributed in my earlier life to my craving for possessions. And it always amazes me that, when the urge to go outside is so strong on the first beautiful spring weekend, some people respond to that urge by going out to a midday dinner in a dark restaurant.

If our private spaces have a tendency to separate us from the natural world, our business spaces are far worse. The design of most offices is not just a question of thrift and functionality. To me some of the most luxurious and status-conscious offices are the most depressingly unnatural. The scale is too large and too geometric with unpaned windows that do not open—if there are windows at all. Whenever I enter a large hotel and go to a function room with no windows, a part of me vanishes. I tend to eat my way into oblivion there, indulging a compulsion that is not unlike the craving for possessions I experienced in the absence of real natural beauty.

FINDING A WAY

Women have been creating good spaces for centuries. These spaces have very often been simple and aesthetic (pleasing to the senses) but rarely ascetic (austere). This is an important distinction because as good an idea as it is to get away from artificial luxuriousness on the grounds that we cannot afford it; it is much better to create a more natural environment because it pleases us. Rather than austerity, we need simple elegance in which the psychic needs of people using a space are reflected and nurtured by the physical surroundings. Beautiful flowers and dramatic color can do as much for the soul as expensive fabric.

A good example of a well-designed natural space is Stephen Gershon's Essex Conference Center on the Atlantic Coast in Essex, Massachusetts. As you first drive up the driveway through the woods and look at the main building, which Gershon built himself (it's obvious at a glance) you are astounded that he could draw businesspeople to this location, but he does. Everything is very simple, even odd, but when you go inside you see that it works. The large meeting space has windows on two sides, and its two other walls are built around huge boulders. This inclusion of the natural earth in the conference room is spectacular. Upstairs, in the dining area, you are served the most extraordinary home-cooked food, buffet-style, seated at long tables with benches; each table seems to be the center of lively conversation and laughter. This is a place where you can definitely stay awake for a conference. Through a multitude of windows you can see the trees and the weather all day long from wherever you are working.

The physical space in which we work, and the furnishings and artifacts that we bring into that space, can have a dramatic impact on what we produce. I led a medicine wheel at an East Coast retreat for a business organization in which the desired goal was to delve as deeply as we could into our mutual understanding of what is needed in business to create a truly sustainable future. The setting was a lovely one-room cottage at a retreat center in New York only an hour outside of the city. The cottage had warm wood walls, big easy chairs and pillows, and a giant stone fireplace on the south side. It was a balmy, but just a touch brisk September weekend. At the end of the day Saturday, I reflected on the very rich day we had had, and I thought, What else can these people possibly say to each other?

On Sunday when people came into the cottage, I had the medicine wheel constructed on the floor. About ten feet in diameter, it contained an outer circle of sixteen stones, with four pathways connecting to an inner circle of seven stones. Artifacts such as a bowl of water or a cluster of leaves marked the four directions, north, south, east, and west. Some Native American flute music played in the background; while a crisp but gentle breeze circulated through the open windows. The morning sun illuminated the room, and a fire was burning in the fireplace. I could feel the impact of the sight, sound, and air on people as they entered the room. The level of meditation and sharing went much deeper than I could have hoped for, and I know it was the space that evoked it.

LINKING THE TANGIBLE AND THE INTANGIBLE

As I said earlier, the feminine affinity for experiencing reality as an integrated whole, as opposed to separating mental and physical space, leads women to pay attention to how their intangible intention—whether it be to develop a mission statement, a strategic plan, or new relationships—relates to the tangible space in which the activity occurs. We know what this sense of place means in the domain of romance; for example, restaurants and other entertainment facilities go to extraordinary lengths to provide the appropriate "atmosphere." If we can get beyond what we think is expected in our business culture, we can introduce some interesting new elements—perhaps guerrilla-style, one small hit at a time—until we all discover how much better working and meeting places can be compared to the windowless hotel rooms, conference rooms, and function rooms we have to endure.

I had an interesting personal struggle with this issue during the year that my parents turned eighty. I felt like a real nuisance to my family as we tried to plan the celebration. I was unenthusiastic about a restaurant setting, ostensibly because cash flow was tight, but that really wasn't it. I wanted this event to be more than a meal. I wanted good psychic space and good physical space and couldn't figure out how to get either.

Together we came up with an unusual idea that took my parents completely by surprise. In a minibus, with my preteen niece and nephew serving as trip attendants, passing out coffee and goodies, we took a three-hour morning tour through my parents' childhood neighborhoods. We stopped at the church where they had been married, found the tennis court where they had first met, passed by their first apartment, and—the grand finale—got a tour of the home in which our entire family had lived for twenty-five-odd years, and in which all my siblings and I had grown up. With easy access to a microphone, we told stories all the way.

By the time we got to lunch at the restaurant, a wonderful stage had been set. All the conversation was about my parents' lives, and the luncheon became the container for the conversation, not the main event. Also, in terms of scale, a luncheon rather than a dinner seemed perfect. The tour and the memories and the breaking of bread were in balance.

When I think of beautiful physical space I always think of my friend Sydney Rice's colonial home north of Boston. Whether you are in her living room or the office space that houses her business, The Coaching Company, you get the same feeling of aliveness.

Sydney cannot live or work in a place that is not visually pleasing. She needs windows and air and a desktop big enough for both stacks of paper and flowers. There is always something living in her space. She prefers a lot of lamps and natural light and can't stand fluorescents. What women used to do, she says, involved moving around—engaging in one activity after another, such as weaving or cooking. In her consulting work she retains a similar pattern. First she dives into some work intensely, then she putters, and then she dives in again.

Sydney's internal space is like my garden. It is very much alive, reflecting her love of what it contains. She says that she takes spaces that she likes and makes them more of what they already are. She loved the sunniness of her living room and the subtle off-green color, so she found things to complement and enhance both. She made linen curtains for their washed look, their natural warmth. She added a beige and white couch, a paprika-colored love seat and brass fixtures. She found some fabric to cover an antique chair that brought together the green and the red so that the chair looked like it belonged. She wanted to make this room inviting in winter as well as in summer. In the winter, she says, what you see is the warmth of the reds and the brass; in summer you notice the white background and cool green. Throughout her home there is a lot of rich pigment, but also many light shades—beige, putty and mushroom, off-white, and cream.

Eighty percent of our awareness comes from our eyes, she points out, so it is no wonder that a building—whether residential or commercial—shapes the kind of thinking that can occur within it. Banks, Sydney observes, convey that they are strong and safe through pillars and marble and counters in front of their tellers. The massive City Hall building in Boston, she feels, makes people seem small, but its odd upside-down shape also embraces them. It conveys omnipotence but also innovation. Massachusetts, it suggests, is a forward-looking state.

Sydney has a keen eye for the intangible message that a tangible space communicates. One office she has seen, she noted, is decorated in an icy blue. To her it felt like it had no heartbeat. Even the mahogany looked cold. In another office she knows, the senior executive offices line a carpeted hall with mahogany walls, but the offices are cubicles with no windows, and they are removed from the support staff—no living things, no windows, not inclusive, she says. She once saw an ice-cream chain that was decorated in black and "poison" green, a marked contrast to Ben and Jerry's homey cows and earth decor. A native of Los Angeles, the center of the entertainment industry, Sydney thinks that East Coast cities understand very little about presentation, about theater.

Talking with Sydney reminds me that there is *always* a link between the intangible and the tangible, for better or for worse. Some buildings do not just lack good aesthetics; they actually convey something else—coldness, intimidation, confusion, conflict, monotony. Consciously or unconsciously physical space reflects and then influences the mind-set of its inhabitants.

At Sydney's suggestion, I visited Lois Silverman's office on the waterfront in Boston. Lois is the chair of CRA Managed Care, Inc., and her Boston office is the headquarters for her national company, which helps injured workers get back on their feet and into productive work.

The company refurbished an old wharf building, sandblasting the brick walls and leaving large wooden beams exposed. Lois's office takes up a corner of the building facing the harbor. The immediate feeling you get as you enter her office is one of warmth, but just as important is the feeling of orderliness and energy. The room is not quite square, approximately twenty by seventeen feet. It is more like a very short, fat L than a rectangle. The two interior walls, rug, and couch are off-white. The two exterior walls are brick, and the oak trim around the door and windows is a warm, light shade, as is Lois's desk, which is set at an angle in the far corner facing the door. The placement of the desk gives the office a sense of movement, of the mobility of its occupant. The large vertical windows, which *do* open, give ample natural light, onto a partially carved bookcase, which is built into and takes up the better part of one interior wall. The bookcase came from Lois's home and is also painted off-white, although it is mahogany underneath. Painting mahogany off-white might appall a lot of people, but not me. A huge green plant, one that looks well cared for and thriving, stands next to the door, and there is a huge vase of fresh cut flowers on the coffee table in front of the couch.

The first thing Lois did when I entered the room was walk around from the desk and sit with me in one of the black chairs that face the desk. She talked about how she built her office and pointed out several gifts that she had on display, items such as clocks and vases that added accent colors to the bookshelves. Like Sydney, Lois likes a lot of light in her office—light-colored walls and/or trim and good windows. It was also important to her to have the right balance between calmness and energy in her space, and enough seating for the people who enter. We both agreed that her off-white rug and her painted mahogany bookcases were a bold move for an office. White, she observed, is "not readily accessible." It may be very soft, but there is a message, too, to tread lightly. My mind immediately went to the idea of diffuse awareness, to the subtle, inclusive characteristic of feminine perception. White contains all the colors, but you cannot see any of them individually. In almost every woman's space I have observed, there is a balance between some version of white, cream, or off-white and strong accent colors, particularly greens and reds.

THE PROBLEM OF LANGUAGE

Whole books and innumerable magazine articles have been devoted to the beautiful, natural spaces women and men have created in which to work and live. I have enormous confidence in our creative capacity to design more beautiful spaces and to bring far more of the natural world into the workplace than we have at the present time. I believe the reason we do not do more designing of our own work environments, more than window dressing that is, has to do with our belief that things have to be the way they currently are in order to be credible.

It is normal for all of us, men and women alike, to accept the existing cultural arrangements within which we live. But when it comes time for questioning the way things are in the public sphere, it is especially difficult to give voice to our feminine sensibilities. As Robert Stein says, the feminine is "not communicated by word or rite but by presence and being" (Stein 1973, 73). We like being with people we consider to be wise, even when they are not speaking, and it is their depth of being that gives meaning to their words. Similarly the private spaces we create communicate without words what we are and what we value. There is no doubt in my mind that we know what we value and what we believe to be true, but it can be difficult to explain *why*. Since explaining *why* is a critical part of current public debate— in business and elsewhere—the inability to articulate our beliefs can stop us from bringing into the workplace not only our feminine aesthetic sensibilities but many of our other feminine capabilities as well.

Therefore I want to take some time here at the end of this section on feminine patterns of work to shed as much conscious light as I can on the feminine problem with language. When I refer to language, I am talking about language as a conceptual tool, the word or rite by which meaning is communicated, not language as an expressive tool, with which the feminine is quite at home.

When I think of language as a conceptual tool, I am reminded of a dream I had in which a young man says to a young woman that she doesn't have to use his material for her presentation, but that she *does* have to use his microphone. At the time that I had this dream I was experiencing a lot of resistance to speaking. I wrote then that I could tell when I had gone deep into my own feminine material because of the reluctance of my mouth to open. I was obsessed with the notion that the essential feminine cannot be put into language. Or more accurately, it seemed that in order to describe my experiences of the feminine, I had to move into the masculine domain of focused consciousness, and I couldn't seem to do so without disconnecting from my feminine source. In another dream sequence around the same time, a young girl did not want to come out of the water to expose herself. I didn't blame her.

Yet a doubt lingered. If something cannot be put into language, is it real? Could I trust what I could not articulate? In the world of action and reaction, I could not hold onto my silent depths as I first began to explore them. It was appropriate then to wait until I became more conscious of my material. But in the long run, this struggle to articulate what I was experiencing was central to me. My desire to learn how to speak about the feminine in terms that did it conceptual justice was at the core of my being. I was deeply touched every time I read a section of Max DePree's *Leadership Is an Art*, the gift of his long years of experience at Herman Miller. To me, the essence of what I consider feminine presence and being permeates his book. The book is so direct and simple that it sometimes seems to be without substance at all. "The first responsibility of a leader is to define reality," he writes, for example. "The last is to say thank you." Or, as I have quoted, a leader needs "to distinguish between what is actually healthy and what merely appears to be living" (De Pree 1987, 11, 21). To grasp his image of leadership you have to let go of all the complex organizational ideas you have and just read his sentences over several times until the obviousness of what he is saying can get through all your conceptual filters.

I had the same feeling about an article about Frances Hesselbein, former head of the Girl Scouts. The article was about her ingenious circular organizational structure. "To those in search of the 'secret' of Hesselbein's genius," the article said, "here is a clue. Her first ambition was to be a poet. A poet must embrace many tasks, not the least of which is making all the parts of a poem fit the whole. The fidelity, in other words, is not to the exquisite turn of phrase but to the essence of the poem" (O'Toole 1990, 28). I thought this was a remarkable description of the essence of a poem. Like other forms of writing, the poem is crafted with words, but it is the relationship *between* words—the tone and ambiance that is created by the combination of words rather than the individual words or phrases—that conveys the meaning of the poem. Similarly, one can use words to describe the feminine, but no one word or phrase can sum up the totality of its meaning. Thus in writing or speaking about the feminine I have had to circle around the substance of the feminine until I found the right combination of words to convey the essence that I could intuit. This is a very different task from using words in the focused consciousness way of conceptualizing or analyzing a subject.

The most difficult task for me still remains consciously distinguishing between using the microphone of my inner masculine focused consciousness and using his material. In her analysis of the fairy tale "The Handless Maiden," Marie Louise von Franz describes how the maiden is given a pair of artificial hands by her husband. According to von Franz, these hands represent the woman's taking on the worldview of her husband, who as a king is the symbol of "a collective, dominating positive attitude." She takes the new hands rather than develop her own worldview. We all have a piece of this woman within us, the one who is conventionally brilliant, who is dutiful, who learns all the skills and adapts. As von Franz says, "[she] behaves normally, but not spontaneously" (von Franz 1972, 83).

The microphone of the young man in my dream represents the capacity to use language conceptually. This is something that I need. But his material, what I largely learned in school and from the public world of men, is something I need to be conscious of and question, deciding bit by bit what to make my own and what to let go. Yet the microphone and the material are so entwined in my past experience that it is difficult to separate the message from the medium.

Reading through my old journals and correspondence is an enlightening experience. I can see the shift in my writing. The older the entry, the clearer "his" voice is; the more recent the entry, the more the voice seems to be that of my real feminine self. We are gradually becoming friends, this inner masculine and I. From time to time he actually hands the microphone over to me quite graciously without speaking at all.

This problem with language, with formulating the true voice of the feminine, is not something to be passed over lightly. There have been, and will continue to be countless instances in our business lives when we will discount ourselves as inadequate when we cannot speak quickly what we really perceive and feel. We will opt for the more conventional use of language, we will decide that we are wrong, or we will decide that we have nothing to contribute. We do these things all the time. Keeping this very real problem in mind is important as we move next to a consideration of feminine leadership. We need to create space and time to prepare ourselves if we are going to give the world the feminine context and content that it really needs from us.

SUMMING UP

Each work pattern in this section reflects back to one or more aspect of the feminine principle discussed in Part 1. The feminine

pattern of sorting information and organizing action most directly reflects diffuse awareness. The expression of deep feeling
and radical trust reflect the feminine affirmation of life as well as
acceptance of its cycles. Mothering and being mothered reflect
both affirmation of life and an awareness of deep community, as
does sensibility about space.

It is possible to sum up everything we have discussed so far
in a conceptual outline, but one of Hesselbein's poems would
probably do it better. By now the image of an energy field is
probably a more accurate description of what is forming in
your mind about the feminine principle. For some readers
diffuse awareness is what stands out in this field. For others
presence and being is more important. For still others deep
community, the quick of the moment, or radical trust are most
memorable. Like pockets of energy or light, these ideas or
phrases stand out as we discuss them and then recede—like stars
in a bright evening sky as we move our eyes from one part of
the heavens to another—giving us a progressively fuller, more
three-dimensional picture of the whole field. This is the best
way to approach the feminine principle. It *can* be understood,
but it defies our focused consciousness and its yearning for full
articulation.

How does one take such amorphous context and content
into the world? In other words, how does one provide truly
feminine leadership when feminine and leadership seem to be
contradictions in terms in our focused consciousness world?
This challenge will be the subject of Part 3.

Part 3

Feminine Leadership

Chapter 10

Honoring Our Feminine Depths

We argue with ourselves: "I should be doing something useful. But the truth is I can't do anything useful if there's no *I* to do it." . . . That is what going into the chrysalis is all about—undergoing a metamorphosis in order one day to stand up and say *I am*.

—MARION WOODMAN, *The Pregnant Virgin*

What is feminine leadership? The first image that comes to mind is women in positions of leadership—presidents, vice presidents, and managers—in existing economic structures. What I mean by feminine leadership, however, is leadership in bringing the feminine principle into our public life. These two definitions for feminine leadership will naturally overlap, but the first does not necessarily include the second. When I began to approach male friends at senior levels in corporations to talk about the traits and skills they perceived in women colleagues, at least one very sensitive man surprised himself by observing that the only women he could think of who were really successful had taken on the traits of men.

In the privacy of their own minds these women undoubtedly share the perceptions and feelings of all women, so that in subtle, and sometimes not so subtle, ways feminine energy is finding its way into the public sphere through their actions. But there is still a great danger that we will think that having women in positions of power is enough, when it is the integration of the *feminine principle* that will really contribute to the creation of a more balanced culture. Eventually this means that integration needs to happen in both women and men, however differently that integration might occur.

THE OPEN TRACK

When I think of the difficulties of bringing the feminine principle into business, I am reminded of my introduction to stock-car racing a few years back. On a summer night in Barre, Vermont, you can hear the drone of Thunder Road long before you can see the spectacle. This, as you can imagine, was not my first idea of entertainment, but I went to be with friends and found that the racing captured my interest far more than I expected it would. You sit high on a hill overlooking mountains in the distance and watch dozens of cars travel at absurd speeds around a quarter-mile track accompanied by the tremendous roar of engines; the periodic pileups are dramatic and exciting, and occasionally hilarious. For some reason I could never fully explain to you, no one seems to get hurt.

On Labor Day, the professionals gathered for a hundred-lap race. For long periods there was just the mesmerizing drone and flash of cars going by. But then, in what seemed like a split second, the first five cars changed positions, and there was a spontaneous roar from the crowd and a rush of adrenaline. I am not even sure that I saw it happen, but I was aware that someone had made a dangerous move and it had paid off. He was now in the lead. I realized that the driver was now experiencing something very different from what he had experienced before he made his move. As the third car back, his task had been to follow the lead car and look for an opportunity to break away. Someone else had been setting the pace. Now he was responsible for setting the pace himself. He still did not have the power to determine the general direction of the course, or when the race would be won, but there was no one out in front of him to take in and sort through the critical information he needed in order to decide how to take the turns and at what speed. In short, the primary job of determining what was real on the track was now his.

For the next forty laps or so I thought about very little else besides what had just happened. I felt in my body a strong identification with this driver. My fascination with this scenario could only mean that in some essential way in my life I had stopped following a lead car. Now I experience nothing out in front of me but open track. I cannot change that track, just as I cannot change life itself, but now I have to make my own observations about what is real and set my own course and pace.

The open track I find myself staring at is feminine leadership. There are very few models out in front to follow. This is true not only because of the times in which we are living, but also because the essential journey to one's inner feminine core is totally unique for each person. As the quote that opens this chapter suggests, Marion Woodman has written extensively about this inner journey, about how the deep feminine within becomes conscious. She uses the image of the chrysalis, the cocoon from which the butterfly emerges, to describe a complex process, applying as much to men as to women, a process that is a lot more like an initiation than a training (Woodman 1985). A great deal of patience is required, along with a flexible time frame, because the duration of the journey cannot be determined in advance.

Working in my garden is one way that I engage in this inner process. I wrote earlier that my garden has helped me to become conscious of my diffuse awareness. My garden generally has become a pathway to my own feminine reality, helping me grasp the "I" that I truly am. More like a field than a laser point, the diffuse awareness of my psyche is easier for me to understand when I can walk outside my door and wander in a *real* field, both the wild one on my hill with its knee-high grass and wildflowers, and the more cultivated one that I have created with my perennials. The horizontal expanse dissipates that in me which is too concentrated and thus overwrought, and the gentle movement of living things in the breeze settles me down and refreshes my spirit.

This is the kind of activity that I find necessary to be able to honor my feminine depths—wandering in fields and woods and in my own psyche. It is not the kind of activity that is readily available to people who are climbing the corporate ladder or building a business, but I have not yet known one woman who has truly come to herself who has not had to take time out, often at inconvenient times, to go deep. Nor have I known many men who have not had to go through an equivalent process to come into their true power. This inner work of self-revelation, as an aspect of the development of feminine leadership, is the focus of this chapter.

THE MILLER'S DAUGHTER

A most exquisite description of this inner work can be found in Marie Louise von Franz's *The Feminine in Fairy Tales*. In one of the tales that she analyses, there is a miller, who, finding himself in financial difficulties, agrees to sell to the devil what is behind his mill. He thinks that he is giving up only an apple tree, but later, to his chagrin, he finds that he has promised his daughter. After three years the devil comes to claim the daughter, but she manages to foil him by washing herself with water, since the devil has no power over water. When the devil takes the water away, she cleans her hands by weeping on them. When the devil cuts off her hands, she cleans her arms by weeping on *them*, and the devil finally gives up. But the damage to the girl is done: she has lost her hands and has become the handless maiden, giving the tale its title.

The maiden's parents are grief-stricken, but they are not able to help her, so she leaves them and wanders out into the world, where her beauty attracts the attention of a king whom she marries, and who gives her a pair of artificial silver hands. Later the king goes off on a mission, and the queen is left alone with her child and her mother-in-law. The king sends messages, and she responds, but the devil intervenes and switches these messages, so it appears that the king has ordered that his wife be killed. To avoid this fate, she goes off into the woods with her child, where she has to deal with her loneliness. It is only through this process that she is able to grow back her own hands.

You can read this tale in a number of ways. It has rich implications for Western culture about selling our feminine side to the devil generally, and the story is well worth reading for that interpretation alone. But the tale interests me more because it explains certain behavior patterns that I recognize in myself and in other women—both the excessively strident traits of some business women and the excessive caution and indecisiveness of others. Inside the story of what the miller does to his own internal feminine, then, there is also the story of the daughter who, von Franz says, "is now living under the shadow of this problem" (von Franz 1972, 79). For me this means that as women take on leadership roles in the world of business, which has largely been designed by their fathers and their fathers' fathers, they have to deal with the absence of the feminine in that domain generally, and also with an almost total lack of understanding of how to use masculine skills appropriately and in respectful harmony with their predominantly feminine psyche.

The hands in this tale represent the woman's ability to act in the world, and in Jungian terminology, this would involve the masculine part of her psyche. The woman's handlessness keeps her out of worldly activity altogether, because as a result of her experience with her father, she does not trust herself not to fall into the devil's hands. Von Franz cites examples of women who have become so obsessed with masculine activity that they have finally decided that their only other choice was total passivity. These women were unable to integrate the masculine and feminine parts of their psyches. Either the masculine became demonic and controlled their lives, as we occasionally see in businesswomen who seem to have lost their touch with the human side of life, or the fight between the two parts of the psyche proved too difficult, so out of fear of this demonic element they retreated into a life of indecision and lack of action.

In this story, the queen deals with this problem in another way. She doesn't become completely passive, because she is given artificial hands by her husband; these new hands, as we saw in the last chapter, allow her to operate from a conventional worldview, but one that is borrowed and not really her own. Acquiring these artificial hands, and living conventionally, might have been the end of the story except for the problem with the mother-in-law, who takes over running the palace while the husband is gone because the queen is not operating autonomously. In the normal patterns of life, a young woman would be able to handle such a competition with an older woman, but this young woman is already wounded in her psyche, having been sold off by her father and made to defend herself against the devil, eventually losing her hands. As a result, von Franz says, "she will not have the energy or ability to defend herself on the outside" (von Franz 1972, 83).

What does it mean not to be able to defend oneself on the outside? That phrase resonates so strongly with me; it brings up remembrances of times when I have stumbled in business situations, unable to make a decision and unable to believe that I was capable of making a decision, even though I had made a thousand decisions before. It reminds me of what several men have reported to me, in real honesty: that although women have great strength in the group process, they have a hard time taking immediate and decisive action when it is called for, and sometimes they have trouble holding their teams accountable for producing results. One senior manager told me that even when women managers know that what is needed in a given situation is to get more input from other people, they have difficulty making the decision to call for that input. His company developed a mentoring program and found that through this program women managers could learn to be more decisive in only six months' time, and the results were long-lasting. In his mind, the problem was not that women were indecisive, but that they had no history of developing their independence as men had. Even getting to interdependence—at which he felt women generally excelled over men—requires going through the stage of independence first.

While I agree with a lot of what he said, I would like to offer a slightly different theory about why women have this difficulty. The women scholars at the Stone Center at Wellesley College showed in *Women's Growth in Connection* (Jordan et al. 1991) that women actually achieve psychological maturity "in relationship." Such relatedness is not perceived by women as being *dependent* but as part of life. In the mentoring program described above, one of the key, though invisible, ingredients might have been that the program gave women permission to be in relationship with their mentors, which, in addition to whatever skills and information they acquired from the program, might have strengthened their confidence enough for their decisiveness to come into play.

Linking this situation back to the story of the miller's daughter, it is important to explore what is the real wound to women that the story represents. In other words, what is the literal meaning in our everyday life of fending off being given to the devil by one's father? It is not really that a woman's masculine skills per se have suffered a blow, but that her feminine essence is discarded in the effort to resolve the world's financial difficulties. Everywhere in business, women have been encouraged to set aside their feminine attributes as at least secondary, if not irrelevant altogether, and to strengthen traditional masculine skills. Yet if a woman cannot esteem the feminine container, which is the primary aspect of her personality, her masculine skills may well appear to be in the devil's hands, because they will be disconnected from her core.

The difficulty that the young woman has with her mother-in-law and the miscommunication with her husband is actually valuable, then, because without these problems the woman would never have gone off into the woods and reconnected with her feminine essence. She would never, then, have been able to grow back her own hands, which represent her authentic ability to act in the world. Such a woman, von Franz says, "will be aware of a dead corner within, . . . for though it looks like she had a husband and children, or a job, she is not yet really alive" (von Franz 1972, 83–85).

Once the devil has interfered between the queen and her husband, the king, she can do nothing but save herself and her child by fleeing into the forest. Here is how von Franz describes the process of the queen's metamorphosis:

> To retire into the forest would be to accept the loneliness consciously. . . . Living in the forest means sinking into one's innermost nature and finding out what it feels like. . . . Frequently women say that the only way in which they can enjoy life a little and not feel so bad over their difficulties is by taking long walks in the woods or by sitting in the sun, . . . it seems as though only nature in its virgin beauty and essence has the power to heal in such a case. . . . Collective standards do not help. She has first to reach the zero point and then in complete loneliness find her own spiritual experience (von Franz 1972, 85–86).

This story has a great deal of personal meaning for me. I sensed for a long time, however unconsciously, that my real task in business, as in life generally, was to find my way back to my feminine core so that I could grow back my own hands. I wanted the masculine part of me to be able to work in the world on my own feminine terms. I have known well that "dead corner within." All of the difficulties and irritations of being a woman in business have prickled and prodded me deeper into a nameless grief. I have been overwhelmed by this grief and not known what it was. It has only been over time that I have learned that this grief was about knowing that I was not known, most painfully, not known to myself.

What I described earlier as stumbling in the making of business decisions was my failure to recognize and validate my feminine essence. It was not that I did not know what I wanted to do. But something in the business environment made me question my judgment so totally that I actually lost touch with the fact that I had any judgment at all. I could sense that I did not view the world in the same way that the men around me viewed it. Instead of standing on my own view—or even looking to see what that view might be—I became enveloped in self-doubt. The end result was paralysis. As a substitute for being able to operate from my feminine core, I have sometimes craved the comfort of collective standards and collective approval, and I still feel disproportionate fear about losing conventional financial security.

But the more I sink into myself and into nature, the more something else grows within for which collective standards are a poor substitute. Here in Vermont, spring takes a long time in coming, but even in March, there is one spot at my back door that is protected and bathed in the sunlight. In front of the door are two woven mats that get warmed by the sun. By noon I can sit out there and feel the sun bake on me and feel profound healing. Across the dirt road the winter snows melt into the brook, whose water races at breakneck speed to the ocean. That sound of running water, combined with the more subtle sounds of running water from the feeder stream on the other side of my house, is stereophonic. Feeling the sun on my face and the earth beneath my body, and hearing that water, I feel alive in a way that I had never experienced before.

I cannot function in the world without these interludes with nature. I need them every day of my life. In the summer I garden; in the winter I carry wood and clear my pond for skating. All year long I cook, and I feed the birds. I feel like I am taking part in an initiation that began a long time ago, the end of which is not yet in sight.

In my business life, looking outside for the problem is no longer my primary focus. When I am most conscious, I know that fixing the existing system to include me is the wrong way to conceptualize the task. Finding a way to include my whole self in my business life *is* the task, and doing so is what will lead me to the level of consciousness I need to create new structures.

NEW CONSCIOUSNESS

An essential aspect of feminine leadership, then, is to find the deep feminine in ourselves *and to make it conscious*. Recently I had a dream in which there was a triangle of three elements of myself: the first was observing, the second was shedding part of itself, and the third was the part that was being shed. Over and over in the dream I was being instructed to pay attention—not only to shed something, but to consciously look back and see what I was shedding.

Realized feminine consciousness, which can only be gained through individual experience, becomes the container within which women's masculine skills can develop and operate in the world without a devilish quality and thus make a real contribution to human life. This development will happen somewhat differently for men, but finding the authentic relationship between the two energies is a central task for all of us.

I do not believe this inner work can be bypassed no matter how competent we become, because making the feminine conscious is a new task we need to undertake for the good of the human species. The feminine is eternally old, but the feminine as a *conscious* partner in the public work of developing civilization has not yet emerged in a form that we can hold in our minds with any clarity and with which we can operate automatically, as most of us, male or female, have learned to do with focused consciousness.

Synapse by synapse, making conscious connections between feminine content and possible ways to structure and work within our systems is painstaking work. This is change at a deeper level than just the mind. We have a million theories and ideas in print that have not begun to touch our real experience of life and thus our behavior. Some indications that change is really

occurring are the presence of emotion—fear, frustration, disorientation, helplessness—and the strange discord we can sometimes feel in our bodies. I have imagined this phenomenon to be
like a spiritual version of a chiropractic adjustment—that split
second when the bone and muscle have moved but have not yet
found their new positions. For months I have felt suspended in
that moment of transition in life and in my business. It is no
wonder that sooner or later I want to engage in *any* action just to
get on with it. Ideas, too, are often in suspension. Theories that I
read that make perfectly logical sense slip out of my memory,
sometimes five pages after I have read them.

It is helpful to know that this is not a new problem. In a
seminar several years back a group of us was discussing the
heavy-handedness of judgment in the Old Testament. The in-
structor offered a surprising interpretation: he said that the harsh
tone of Old Testament patriarchs may have meant that even for
the leaders of the Hebrew people, the concept of a new covenant
with a single God was a fundamentally new way of perceiving
reality. Thus, they were struggling to make their understanding
of this new consciousness real, and the less confident they felt
about the new, the more adamantly they opposed the old, even
while they fell back into old patterns of what they now viewed
as idolatry.

What is the "old" that periodically horrifies us today, even
as we fall back into the old patterns? Our old view of survival,
for one, keeps haunting us. We keep behaving in ways that we
are not yet confident we can afford to let go of; for example, we
make extraordinary efforts to increase and maintain our current
standard of living despite its impact on our environment and on
ourselves. Corruption and deceit, in business and in government, still plague us, and we are increasingly alarmed by
the endless bargaining from self-interest that goes on in our
government and results more and more often in paralysis and
stalemate.

Like the ancient Hebrews of the Bible, we are sometimes
righteous and confrontational about our individual and collec-

tive failure to live up to our own often new and often contradictory standards. There is no precedent, for example, for working within government in any way except through bargaining from self-interest. Nor do we have much information about how to live well outside our consumer-based economy, or about how our government or corporations will survive if they tell the whole truth to the public. We think our problems simply have to do with ethics, or conscience, but it is not that simple; we are dealing with problems of *consciousness* too.

We are not, in terms of our daily practices, where our intuition tells us we need to be. In my own life, as I work toward better alignment between my emerging understanding of reality and the actual way I live on a daily basis, intense feelings often come up from the depths. Since these feelings are not yet fully understood, they are more often terrifying than appealing, especially when I think I don't have *time* for them. Who will mind the store if I fall apart? Thus there is a continual tension between surviving in the world that I know versus taking the time to allow new consciousness to emerge that might, in fact, alter my view of survival.

WHO WILL MIND THE STORE IF I FALL APART?

Inner work is an essential part of the process of change, especially major change. Sufficient inner reflection is critical to counteract and deal with the fear that comes from the unknown. The task of integrating the feminine and the masculine—if honestly undertaken—makes demands on the individual that are outside what is expected in terms of conventional business behavior. Many of us are finding that we need to move out of the mainstream of economic life, at least for a while, to reorient ourselves to a new perspective. This is where we find out whether what we have been saying for so long about trusting the universe is just a nice thought or a belief system that can sustain us when we can see nothing positive in the future. Every spiritual system that

I know describes something equivalent to the dark night of the soul. Murray Stein, in *In Midlife*, calls this phenomenon "liminality," that is, the crossing of the threshold, the essential truth being that you cannot see across the threshold to where you are stepping (Stein 1988, 8–9). The Celtic runes call it "leaping, empty handed, into the void" (Blum 1982).

For many people, liminality is an integral part of major change, and that feels very much like death. It may come with a painful layoff, a crisis of conscience within a corporate setting, or they may discover that they can no longer effectively continue what they are currently doing. As I watched my business dwindle a year or so ago, along with my interest in it, I felt repeatedly assaulted by the feeling that I was unsuited to public life, either political or economic. In such moments I felt that my credentials were all a façade. Behind the straight As, the cum laude Ivy League degree, the government jobs, the ownership of a business, and so forth, I was a person for whom the world of conventional business made about as much sense as the workings of a car underneath the hood. As I looked back over my life, it seemed that I had plodded my way through all these things— doing well at school, being successful at a job, and starting a business. I could see that I had grown up in a time when women believed that the *real* work belonged to men in the public sphere, so I had talked myself into enthusiasm for it. Quite simply, it had looked like "life" to me, and I had not wanted to miss out.

I realized that as I submerged myself in these tasks, it seemed I largely invalidated my inner life and gave myself over to the demands of the outer world. I functioned well enough for a long time because I worked hard at it, never rebelling like my husband did (he told me he concealed the library books he wanted to read inside his required school textbook covers). But as I approached midlife, it got harder to go on living this way, always putting my nose to the grindstone and making things work. When I experienced a major setback in my business, I could no longer muster the imagination to figure out how to put the business right or find the energy to come up with an alternative. In my heart of hearts I knew that all I *really* wanted to do was to read and write, cook, and tend to my garden. To make matters worse, I lived on a dirt road in the country—on a hill, in fact—which takes my full attention to drive six months of the year because of the ice and snow in the winter and the mud in March and April. If I had to, I thought at the time, how would this "flatlander" from Massachusetts even get to a regular job at McDonalds?

I wrote that last line knowing that it would provoke a laugh, but the truth is that my situation was very painful. Did I really have to choose between having what felt like a real life to me and earning a living? This was not about laziness; the physical and mental energy I put into my garden was as intense as any a new CEO could give to a fledgling enterprise. Rather, something seemed very much out of whack between the options my culture offered me and the needs of my human psyche to have meaningful work in my life.

Looking back over my dream journal during that time, I see that my dreams were populated by a jumble of snotty, judgmental figures and contained wildly chaotic scenes in which everything was entangled, and nothing could be sorted out—clothes, mostly, but sometimes people and situations too. Routinely in these dreams I couldn't find my shoes, or there were so many pairs to choose from that I couldn't decide which ones to wear. Shoes, I am told, are symbols of one's standpoint, which I never seemed able to find or settle on in these dreams.

The good news from this period of painful psychic upheaval was twofold. First, something from within had gripped me that I will never be able to shun again. Simply putting my nose to the grindstone and earning money was no longer going to be a satisfactory path, even a possible path. Secondly, having gotten myself into the thick of business, I carry in my brain some knowledge and appreciation of what a great many people are struggling with—both the stress of inhumanly busy schedules and the dissatisfaction with the work that fills their long workweeks. This knowledge helped me to feel less alone even in the most lonely moments. It also focused my mind on exploring new patterns of living not just for myself but for everyone. The bad news was that the future looked bleak, empty, without form, and most poignantly, without financial resources. I no longer hoped for a quick reprieve, a new idea that would come out of the blue in response to my good intentions. Instead I had a new respect for the hard work I would have to do to restructure my life, with nothing but the blind threshold of liminality in front of me.

I know that many other people have had similar experiences, including many men. One Fortune 500 company executive told me about how life started to change for him. Attending a training in the mid-1980s, he somehow tapped into an experience of an inner spiritual part of himself that he had not known before. "There was just no going back," he says. He then found himself gravitating toward what he perceived as the feminine in himself: he became more intuitive, more oriented toward group participation, more caring about what happened to other people, and more inclined to tell the truth about issues concerning people, including customers. In the early 1990s this career corporate executive left his job and, according to him, within a six-month period "everything in my life that I was attached to exploded." Still in liminality today, he has traveled a good deal, lived in a spiritual community, and is now tending a farm as a caretaker. I wish I could tell you that he now operates his own multimillion-dollar company that operates on a set of standards perfectly balanced between the masculine and the feminine, but for most of us, that pathway has not yet revealed itself.

SAVING THE CHILD

I tell these stories because I want to underscore again my belief that this inner work is an essential part of the process of change. It is not just for someone else. Although there is no prescribed pattern—no knowing what the path to the inner depths will be for any individual—there will be at least one time in each of our lives, probably many, when we will have a choice to go deep into our real or symbolic forests to deal with our loneliness and find our own spiritual experiences. Very few of these individual encounters will be convenient—since we won't be able to plan them in advance—but if we carry forward what we learn, cumulatively these experiences can make an enormous difference to our consciousness and, ultimately, to our work.

The end of the story of the miller's daughter gives us a clue about how significant this difference in consciousness and work could be. In some versions of the tale the queen grows new hands when she reaches into a well to save her drowning child. Wanting to "save the child," says von Franz, is often the only thing that will draw some women into this kind of healing. The child does not literally have to be a child. It could be anything one is passionate about. As I reread this part of the story, I was struck by how many of my friends, both men and women, are working to transform business or protect the environment. Perhaps for many of us, the child that is drowning and thus drawing us toward our own spontaneous work is the earth itself.

This line of thought brings me back to the original problem of the miller, which was that he sold his soul, his feminine anima, to the devil to get out of financial difficulty cheaply. As we face very real and possibly irreversible threats to our biosystem, it seems that we are frantically trying to get out of these difficulties cheaply. We seem unable to grapple with the contradictions between the details of our daily lives and our desire for a sustainable future: continuous worldwide distribution of goods, which consumes large quantities of fuel, when we have the option to develop a more sensible system of regional distribution; putting out reams of paper that consume trees and other sources of energy; or in general producing, marketing, and accumulating massive quantities of nonbiodegradable things.

Perhaps the only way we will break this pattern, which seems to have such a grip on the entire industrial world, is if one by one we work through our fear and grief. This is the pathway that can evoke the deep love we spontaneously have for the child we call earth. Thus, more than counseling us to be responsible and dutiful, the story of the miller's daughter suggests that we need to find the passion within for which all our collective standards and cravings will be a poor substitute. Feminine leadership, then, is not just the assumption of power by women in our existing institutions, but the formulation of a different kind of power base—one that comes from the authentic feminine passion deep within us—a foundation that will inform everything we do in business.

Once we have found our feminine passion, then we are ready for a truly original and creative collaboration between masculine and feminine energy—both within our psyches and in the world. Here again, we are faced with an open track where we have no choice but to set our own course and pace. The next chapter offers us some images that can help us with this challenging opportunity.

Chapter 11

Collaboration with the Masculine

The woman who is in touch with her inner virgin has passed the frontier of the anima woman operating out of male psychology. She finds herself saying things she never said before, verbalizing questions she never asked before. She tries to speak from her feminine reality while at the same time aware of the masculine standpoint. Often she is caught between two conflicting points of view: the rational, goal-oriented, and just, versus the irrational, cyclic, relating. Her task is not to choose one or the other, but to hold the tension between them.

—MARION WOODMAN, *The Pregnant Virgin*

In the early 1990s, a group of twelve of us were hosting an annual meeting of a business organization that was in considerable pain. Our goal was to help the members work through a great deal of conflict and confusion about the organization's purpose, and we were not sure that we could succeed. All twelve of us participated in facilitating the meeting at various times over the three days of the conference, but one particular man and I ended up as the point people who coordinated the planning and kept the program moving once it was in progress.

This was the first time I had collaborated so closely with one man on something that really mattered to me, other than in my personal life or my business. Two months before the conference, the whole twelve-person team met to design the overall program. From that point on, my male colleague and I coordinated the preparations for the meeting. I was the one through whom all information flowed; I also set up and managed the deadlines. I communicated with anyone who needed to know what someone else was doing, and encouraged similar conversations among others. My male colleague, on the other hand, was more focused on the end result. He would call me to express some concern about where someone might be going astray or where we might run into a time problem. Everything he observed was accurate and very helpful to me.

Once we got to the conference, all twelve of us on the original team met together at least once a day to communicate with each other about how the program was going. My male counterpart was the main facilitator, taking the first and last sessions and several critical sessions in the middle. Various other facilitators took over for one or two sessions at a time. We laughed a lot about behaving like a flock of geese in flight. That V-shaped formation of the geese has a purpose. The lead goose has the brunt of the work, and those that follow can fly more easily. Thus they take turns. And so did we: after doing a stint as lead goose, each could drop back and follow with the rest.

Throughout the conference I watched the pacing of the sessions and monitored our progress. I intervened at one point and suggested alternative ways for people to follow up with each other when an otherwise excellent session went far too long and jeopardized our ability to get to the heart of the program. The whole ambience of the conference was what I focused on, what some people might call the "space." "Space," of course, includes the overall physical environment—the interaction between presenters and participants that the physical setup allows, encourages or discourages; the length of the sessions; the timing of breaks; keeping on schedule, and so on. But the idea of space also includes the psychological environment—in this case whether or not people felt emotionally comfortable with the exercises and whether or not our program excited sufficient energy and was relevant for the participants, so that they could be authentic and commit themselves to the work. Since comfort and energy levels can change at any moment, the intangible "space" required continuous monitoring and maintenance. As I stayed focused on that aspect of the conference, my male colleague, like a laser beam, could stand in the center of the circle and, with blunt honesty and humor, engage the group in its work.

Later he told me how *he* had viewed the experience. He thought that I had stabilized the planning group initially and brought everyone around to agreement on a goal. I was not nearly as conscious of the stabilization role I had played as he was. Once the goal was established, and he felt confident that the process was the right one, he said, it was easy for him to do the work that he did.

A second factor, he observed, was that he could see the conflicts coming. He was a decade older than most of us and had experienced working in a large company—of four hundred or so partners with different agendas. He understood, therefore, that within a group one could encounter not just one, but multiple conflicts. He was both far more realistic than I about the resistance members would have to our ideas, and more optimistic about ultimately resolving the conflict.

His savvy on this score was certainly based on experience, yet I suspect it also had something to do with gender. A woman entrepreneur told me about a similar dynamic with her partner. When they do waste management audits for hospital clients, she is the one who picks up on the almost tribal dynamics within the hospital organization, but he is the one who can see that some of the biggest barriers to their program can be the biggest opportunities. For example, he could see that if you can identify with a top administrator and explain the benefits from his point of view, that administrator can become your greatest champion. In my experience, most men seem to understand this better than most women do.

Now, the hard part is telling you *exactly* what my male colleague and I actually did together in that conference. It is easier to give the broad outline as I did above, and to say that I felt enormous synergy. To a greater extent than ever before, I felt able to surrender to a dynamic interaction, which I could feel but could not fully understand or master by myself. I did not truly know what my colleague would bring to bear on a particular session. At several points he told a poignant personal story that was not on the agenda—and may not have even been on his mind before he stood up—but that was just exactly what was needed.

I trusted that if I kept my mind clear about the end result we desired, I would know what was appropriate to do or say in the moment, and so would he. Thus, though I was an equal player, I did not control the game—an experience I found both unsettling and very exhilarating. We were both totally tuned in to what was happening in front of us, but we were providing different kinds of energy, neither of which would have been sufficient to hold the whole group together.

This experience was not the same as some others I have had which I call teamwork, where everyone is working at essentially the same task. Nor did it have the natural flow of working with a group of all women. The twelve of us on the planning team knew what our goal was, and we did have a plan, but we had only the vaguest idea of what content and energy would really work to get the organization's members to the level of alignment that we hoped to achieve.

What happened was really a spontaneous creation, not an implementation of a plan. When I look back on the experience, it seems to me that as far as my male colleague and I were concerned, what happened was an example of what is possible when masculine and feminine energy trust each other and respond moment by moment to support each other—just like good choreography.

MASCULINE/FEMININE CHOREOGRAPHY

More than with anything else that I have written in this book, I have struggled with how to describe what I would call really good choreography between masculine and feminine energy in business. I use the image of choreography because it is dynamic, conveying the perpetual motion of creation, the strength and participation required of each partner, and the need for each partner to have the utmost respect for the other's work.

Gaining mastery is a joint effort, just as in a marriage; each partner is responsible for his or her own action, but that individual action occurs within the context of the relationship. After sixteen years in business with a man who is my partner in life as well, I still find it difficult to articulate what actually happens between us. I hope that the few examples you find in this chapter will stimulate your memories and your future observations so that together we can convey to our sons and daughters—in sufficient detail to be helpful—how this masculine-feminine partnership can work in business.

When I think of good choreography between the masculine and feminine, I always think of pairs figure skating. In 1980, when I was first starting my business, I started announcing to my business partners in early January that I was not working nights or weekends for two solid weeks that February. If you have ever started a business, you know full well how loudly you have to make such pronouncements for anyone to take you seriously. In a start-up situation, the company can own you as thoroughly as the Marine Corps owns a recruit in boot camp. But I was determined to block out this time for myself, and there was only one possible event that could command my attention to this degree: the Winter Olympics. That year, I was sure, Tai Babilonia and Randy Gardner were going to take the gold medal in pairs figure skating from the Russians.

They didn't. Not because they were not the best skaters in the world, but because Randy sustained an injury that made it impossible for the pair to compete. I cried for days, at least as much for myself as for them. For years I had been following them, mesmerized by their beauty on the ice. Vicariously I experienced every move they made. I could listen to music for hours with my eyes closed imagining myself gliding over the ice in perfect unison with a partner and spinning gracefully in the air high above the rink.

It is through pairs figure skating that I have come to appreciate choreography, especially the ways in which masculine and feminine strengths complement and support each other. The words of a very young Tai Babilonia, years before she and Randy became U.S. and eventually world champions, ring in my ears every time I watch a pairs competition. With some embarrassment she explained to the television interviewer that her coach had told her that her partner's job was to present her, and that her job was to allow herself to be presented. So as a pair glides across the ice, the figure that draws your attention is the female, and the one who carries her weight is the male. The woman must have muscular control, flexibility, and a good deal of strength of her own, and the male must have the strength to hold her body aloft across the full length of the rink. This requires real power.

Imagine an invisible axis that is the vertical balance point between the two skaters. As each skater shifts up or down on the axis, or farther out or closer in to the axis, the other skater must shift position to maintain balance. This image is similar to the symbol for yin and yang that is also in balance without being symmetrical. In my mind's eye I can see Tai and Randy gliding down the ice with Tai in an overhead position. Depending on the exact position of her body, Randy must use the extension of an arm or leg, or simply lean his body to counterbalance her weight.

In this kind of dynamic movement where balance is essential, the female skater, when she is aloft, complements and supports the male skater by maintaining the balance of her own body in the air. If she leans too far to one side, both of them will topple over. She has to exercise real power of a different sort from her male partner, that is, the power to trust. If the male skater falls, she is likely to land on her head, striking with a force that could cause life-threatening injuries. We are so accustomed to perfect performances on the television screen that we forget that the skaters cannot learn such maneuvers without hours of practice and countless crashing failures. Trusting the masculine action, then, is not necessarily less risky than engaging in that action itself, because the masculine action produces consequences for everyone and everything. And there is certainly feminine action that must accompany that trust, even if it is not so obvious. Few of us have the muscle control or lung capacity of a female skater, both of which allow her to hold the beauty of the lines that she and her partner are presenting to the audience.

This image of pairs figure skating demonstrates that in good choreography between masculine and feminine energy, each has a definitive role to play with its own requirements and complications. When Marion Woodman uses the word "virgin" in the quote that opens this chapter—a word that means "whole and complete," *not* "untouched"—she is referring to the autonomous role that the feminine is called upon to play in the drama of life. The phrase "anima woman" means a female personality that only reflects back to a man his own masculine image of the feminine, not her own version of the feminine (Woodman 1985, 51). As a woman becomes more conscious and appreciative of her authentic feminine core, she gains a new capacity to speak in her own voice; this capacity is unrelated to male impressions of the feminine. Knowing her true feminine value, a woman can then collaborate as an autonomous equal with the masculine— both the masculine within herself, as we discussed in the last chapter, and the masculine in the world at large. The creative collaboration of these forces is the focus of this chapter.

The same is true for men. Some women worried about the emergence of the Men's movement, for example, but to me it was a natural counterpoint to the women's consciousness-raising of the past several decades. The beginnings of such movements in any period of history tend to be erratic, extreme, and strident, but the work that gets done almost always leads to new and deeper consciousness eventually. Seeing Robert Bly and Marion Woodman on video, working with men and women together, gives me hope that a real reconciliation is in our future.

I am actively seeking such a reconciliation in the public domain of work. After so many decades of gender strife, surely there is a reward on the horizon. In the third decade of my marriage, for example, there has descended upon my husband and me an unexpected grace that has made all the work we have done on our relationship worthwhile. We feel this grace daily, breathing new life into our marriage. We are each more balanced between the masculine and feminine than we were when we married in our twenties. But we are also more respectful and accepting of both our own strengths and those of the "other."

THE DYNAMICS OF CONCEPTION

How would we recognize in business an authentic collaboration between the whole, mature masculine and the whole, mature feminine? The willpower and mental capacity to break through old modes of thinking that are associated with masculine energy would be in full play, but those capacities would be rooted in deep community and balanced by an active acceptance of the cycles of life, both of which are qualities associated with feminine energy. Consider, for instance, what occurs during conception as a metaphor for how masculine and feminine energies interplay. What actually happens is counter to our common perceptions.

> Although outwardly the feminine receives and submits to penetration, in the inner invisible mystery of her being she [her ovum] actively dissolves and dismembers [the sperm] in order to re-create; whereas the outwardly aggressive male, in this inner sanctuary, experiences the bliss of surrender to a different kind of wisdom (Whitmont 1984, 137).

The feminine attracts us toward acceptance of and immersion in life; it draws us into those experiences of apparent chaos that evoke the most terror in us, but it also leads us to the "bliss of surrender to a different kind of wisdom." When tragedy or drastic change intrudes upon our lives, we can feel ourselves to be the sperm that is being dissolved and dismembered by the ovum of life. In those moments, we can also experience the re-creation that life is working in us, although we would never have predicted such in our efforts to avoid the turmoil. In those moments of re-creation, people's lives change forever. I see this every day in the experiences of volunteers in my community, like my husband, who work on the ambulance squad. When they are holding the life or death of a person in their hands, especially when they are witnessing and accepting the death of someone they know, ordinary time and ordinary events seem to stop, and the full mystery of life wordlessly envelopes their consciousness.

It is quite clear in these life-changing situations that we are not in charge, however much we may be the actors in the drama. In sexual intercourse, the situation is similar: the masculine sperm is what we always consider to be the initiator. Up to a point it is, but in the actual moment of conception, the mysterious feminine ovum initiates the transformation. The role of initiation is dynamic, and it shifts back and forth; first the masculine initiates, and then the feminine. The role of initiation continues to shift in a dynamic way after conception. While the female gestates, the male protects. When the moment of birth arrives, the female body is in charge, however much we assist with technology.

In the larger scheme of things, we ignore at our peril the dynamic and shifting nature of the role of initiator. We automatically think of the masculine as initiator, yet life itself—the physical world and the bodies in which we live—has been perceived throughout the ages as feminine, and it is to this version of the feminine that we must all ultimately surrender. This does not mean that men should surrender to women personally any more than women should surrender to men personally. Setting up either human feminine energy or human masculine energy as the only legitimate initiating force makes about as much sense as substituting a horizontal board for a vertical board in building a house. The horizontal floors and ceilings won't work very well without the vertical walls, and vice versa.

When I think of the feminine life principle to which we must all surrender, I remember a line from the margarine-versus-butter taste comparison on a television commercial: the actress says, "It is not nice to fool Mother Nature." Then she waves her wand, and there is an ominous sound indicating that some natural disaster is about to take place. Some of the most banal advertising concepts can be the most profoundly, if unconsciously, linked to truth! There is always a price to be paid for trying to fool Mother Nature. In business, for example, the fact that nature will allow herself to be used to produce a wide variety of products does not mean that we can ignore overarching necessities of living systems such as the protection the planet gets from the ozone layer and the need of all living things for a continuous supply of uncontaminated water.

At the human level, feminine energy—in the forms of diffuse awareness, affirmation of life, and acceptance of tumultuous life cycles—is needed in business so that we will constantly raise questions about the relationship between what we are doing and the overall design and needs of the planet. This consciousness is hard to hold onto in the fast pace of business life.

Masculine energy is needed to focus our attention on what needs to be done and to do it. I saw a good example of masculine energy in a workshop I attended. We had gotten off the track in a dialogue about community, and one man inserted himself and spoke with such calmness, magnanimity, and certainty that it brought the room to a great stillness. I told him afterward how much I had appreciated what he had done, how well he had served the overall intent of the meeting. The best of the masculine to me is summed up in the word I would use to describe what this man did: "stewardship," that is, speaking and doing in service to the whole. So many men carry out this role with skill and dedication throughout their work lives.

Once the strategy for action is set, the feminine makes a second form of contribution: containing and orchestrating human energy to accomplish a goal. These activities involve some of the assertiveness of the masculine action, but are subtly different in that they move in the direction of bringing people together rather than leading a charge. After conception is accomplished, for example, the female body becomes the container of the genetic inheritance of both man and woman. A pregnant woman holds the fetus and allows new life to be born through her body, even if it means her own death, which it sometimes does. Then, once the child is born, the feminine actively nurtures by drawing forth the best of the child.

THE FEMININE AS CONTAINER AND ORCHESTRATOR

In managing a family, a community activity, or an office, the people who provide feminine energy are concerned with the context or values that inform the whole operation. They do not decide these alone but are the holders of consciousness about the whole field of human activity and the interrelatedness of its individual parts. They also act as the containers and orchestrators of growth and activity once an action is decided upon. The people who provide masculine energy focus attention on designing and directing the specific action that is required. I have worded this carefully because the providers of feminine energy will sometimes be male rather than female, and vice versa; all of us can play different roles at different times. My point is less about who plays what role than it is about learning to recognize and respect the roles *equally* as they are being played out.

Looking more closely at the feminine role of container and orchestrator, we can see that Marion Woodman is right: one does not choose between "the rational, goal-oriented, and just" of the masculine energy and the "irrational, cyclic, relating" of the feminine energy; instead the idea is to hold the tension between the two. This brings us back to our earlier discussion of the feminine mental capacity to simultaneously include *both* "both-and" *and* "either-or."

A male senior manager told me this story of his five-year partnership with a female assistant who later became an entrepreneur. At the time, this man was an industry manager whose primary task was strategic. His strengths, he says, were intuition, strategy, and decision making. His assistant's strengths were relationship and the day-to-day operations. He also described her as tactical and then realized that what he was describing as tactical was really about relationship; whereas his strategic role had less to do with relationship specifically. In the day-to-day operations "all roads converged with her," he reported, and the boundaries between work and personal problems became blurred as she became known to everyone she worked with as "Mother." As he and his assistant developed and tested their working relationship, each became both more autonomous and more trusting of the other. When he would devise strategy, she would say, "You can't do this, because it will affect x," or "If you are going to do y, you have to do it this way," or "You need to talk to these people, have a meeting with them."

I have a mental picture of this woman in action. She is like so many businesswomen I have met. She knows what is going on with everyone, anticipates what they need, and orchestrates their individual skills and strengths so that they can give their best performance for themselves and for their company. Orchestration involves bringing into harmony the sounds of many different instruments played by many different players, and that is what I can imagine this woman doing with people in her office. And what was at the heart of her ability to do this, I would wager, was the love she had for the people and the process. I would guess that in her own mind she viewed her work less as winning a contest than as producing a great performance, and while the two are not mutually exclusive, the focus of activity is very different.

THE FEMININE AS LOVER

There is an important feminine element behind this scenario. The feminine as container and nurturer of human possibility is also the feminine as lover. No work has ever satisfied me so much as successfully completing a tough project with my staff in which everyone gave one hundred percent. This happened most often in the context of an interminable series of days producing television commercials against a deadline. At the end of each day, we would go out together for a celebration, with good food and lots of laughter about our faux pas. The best part of the evening was when we told endless stories about how each individual had saved the day in his or her unique way. If you have never worked on a television production, you cannot possibly imagine the number of props and gadgets and complicated arrangements that are required on the spur of the moment and that someone has to figure out how to handle.

On other occasions, we would drop everything and rent a limousine to go pick up a sales team at the airport when they had had a particularly successful trip to one of the many cities we visited during the mid-1980s selling advertising space on milk cartons.

How I loved all those people and their work! The feelings I had for them remind me of Psyche's mythical encounter with Eros, during which she discovers his extraordinary beauty. Eros represents the masculine, and Psyche the feminine, so Psyche's discovery of Eros is about her love for the masculine energy and her characterization of that energy as beautiful. I felt precisely that way about my staff—all of them, men and women alike. This deep love for life and for its players—a natural expression of the feminine affirmation of life—is one of the great gifts that the feminine offers to the masculine in any collaboration, in work or in private life.

In addition to actually loving Eros, Psyche becomes *conscious* of her own capacity to love—not just to love an individual man, although that is often how a woman discovers this capacity—but to love all of life. Psyche is simultaneously transformed by her view of Eros—the beautiful, masculine "other"—and her view of herself—as feminine lover, and this second aspect of her transformation is an important part of feminine development. When a person is passionately acting as a container and orchestrator of growth and activity at work, that person is experiencing the same kind of deep love for life that Psyche felt for Eros. But the feminine is only fully *conscious* at work when one experiences the deepest kind of satisfaction from simultaneously knowing oneself as lover and valuing one's work for that reason.

Experiencing oneself as a lover is nicely illustrated in the self-revelation of one Sister Mariana, a seventeenth-century Portuguese nun who wrote to her French soldier lover, "I discovered that it was not so much you as my own passion to which I was attached" (Barreno et al. 1975, 340). A woman who has been in the grip of an all-consuming erotic response knows that life will never be the same for her again. It is as though she has truly impersonated the Goddess, the divine feminine. All of physical life becomes forever permeated with spirit.

As this occurs, a woman paradoxically becomes more whole in herself rather than less so. As much as she loves the man, she is sufficient within herself—that is, her love completes her—and does not need to own him. Even in her most excruciatingly painful moments of loss she knows this. Take, for example, Edith Wharton's Sophie Viner in *The Reef*. As her awareness of what she had in her affair with George Darrow deepens, she accepts her loss of him without recrimination. To Darrow she says,

> Don't for a minute think I am sorry! It was worth every penny it cost. My mistake was in being ashamed, just at first, of its having cost such a lot. . . . I tried to take your attitude about it, to "play the game" and convince myself that I hadn't risked any more on it than you. Then, when I saw you again, I suddenly saw that I *had* risked more, but that I'd won more too—such worlds! (Wharton 1985, 541)

In my mind this is the highest feminine purpose there is, to feel great passion however it comes into our lives and then put this love into the world. Like St. Augustine's passion, feminine passion gets spiritually redirected too, but into the world instead of out of it, or, as Marion Woodman says, the erotic feeling that we usually associate only with sexuality "becomes our total response to the whole world" (Woodman 1982, 188).

I have wondered what motivated those men who have had the most long-lasting successes in public life. I imagine them as impassioned about their work, not just to get power over others and make money, but to contribute something to the human story. This is the true fulfillment of masculine power. It makes sense that women, too, want to contribute something to the human story. Why not through a love so great and so constant that it holds the whole earth system together through times of great change? This may be the way the feminine seeks its own fulfillment. By not acknowledging the real differences between masculine and feminine energy—out of a fear of being relegated to a role that we have been taught to view as weak and unimportant—many of us may fail to find our greatest passion and our greatest work.

Our desire to avoid being stereotyped is directly related to cultural judgments that masculine fulfillment is more valuable than feminine fulfillment. As it stands now, the masculine role of designing and leading the action is the role that we are most conscious of and for which we have the most respect. The feminine role of containing and orchestrating human energy has a fair amount of acceptance and recognition today in business, but it is not regarded as nearly as important or central as the masculine strategic role. And the feminine concern for context—the concern for the whole field of human activity and the interrelatedness of the individual parts—is, in my mind, the weakest link in this dynamic interaction between the masculine and feminine energy in our current business climate. We are often not even aware that this contribution is missing. If we were pairs figure skaters, our balance would have failed by now, and we would have found ourselves sprawled on the ice.

The inner journey to one's feminine core is one track of feminine leadership. Collaborating with the masculine in the outside world is another. In terms of the good choreography that we are trying to establish between masculine and feminine energy in business, most of us are still very much in the discovery and improvisational stage. A friend once said to me that if you saw someone cracking an egg and mixing it in a bowl with flour and shortening and you knew nothing about transforming the mixture through the process of baking, you would be certain that the cook was producing only chaos. Truly integrating the feminine with the masculine in the public sphere may initially be as unsettling to us as cooking might appear to a person who does not understand the process. When I think back to the Humpty Dumpty rhyme, I wonder if the queen might have suggested the simple and shocking idea of using Humpty in a cake, instead of trying to put him back together at all.

Both tracks of feminine leadership—inner and outer—are wide open with plenty of room for any one of us to take the lead. So too is the track we will consider in the next chapter: the track of developing new patterns of work and new organizational structures that more closely reflect our passions and our values.

Chapter 12

Patterns of Change

Throughout history, the really fundamental changes in societies
have come about not from dictates of governments and the
results of battles but through vast numbers of people changing
their minds—sometimes only a little bit.

—WILLIS HARMAN, *Global Mind Change*

I have heard Willis Harman share this basic thought a number of
times. He has also said that as people change their perceptions,
they form small pockets of energy around the globe engaging in
local experiments. Eventually, the sum total of what is learned in
these local experiments will produce the real change that we
need for the world. These ideas give me hope and relieve my
soul from being overwhelmed by the mass media reports that
focus so completely on what is going wrong. The real news, as
Robert Muller said years ago, may not be in the newspapers (or
other media) at all (Muller 1978).

This incremental pattern of change is congruent with feminine consciousness. Diffuse awareness concerns itself with the
broadest possible picture of life by, paradoxically, perceiving
and integrating into that picture the most minute details.

Effective feminine leadership, then, may be found less often in bold and dramatic public action than in small, often out of the mainstream, experiments, the cumulative effect of which may be the fundamental change that Harman describes.

But thinking about the idea of engaging in small, often out of the mainstream, experiments may be more attractive than actually taking one on—at least at first. Early in my exploration of the feminine I had a dream that contrasted two points of access to an island. One was a large pier that extended straight out into the ocean. This was a pier that actually exists on a real island that I know, and it is the only place where people can come ashore on that island. But in my dream there was a second access point on the back side of the island, a smaller pier running parallel to the land instead of perpendicular to it. It was made of warm reddish wood with several slots where boats could dock, instead of the one or at best two places to dock at the central pier.

Now it does not take a psychologist to see the gender imagery in this dream. The dream was clearly inviting me to access the island through a feminine entrance rather than the established masculine entrance. One would expect that I was thrilled by this second pier that had such a wonderful welcoming quality, but in the dream I was very conflicted about using it, because in my experience the larger pier was where all the visible action took place—the comings and goings of ferries and private boats carrying all the people and supplies. At the back side of the island I felt lonely. I found it difficult to choose to be there, because the habits of a lifetime have accustomed me to the action and visibility of the central pier. Action and visibility are deeply embedded in my assumptions about what makes work worthwhile.

Experimenting in small ways outside the mainstream of conventional career wisdom—whether that takes the form of changing your career path to a less glamorous or visibly less powerful one, choosing work that you love over an increase in financial reward, or simply refocusing your goals in your existing workplace to meet your personal desires rather than following what is viewed as the right path in that company—can make you feel invisible and lonely, as if you were landing on that small pier on the back side of the island.

When I reduced the size of my company, I had a difficult time imagining being without my employees, because I loved their camaraderie, but I needed to make that change so I could evaluate what I really wanted my company and my work to be. Ultimately, I found that I loved the solitude at least as much as I had loved the energy of companionship. Others I have known have dreaded leaving a large corporate post for the same reason, only to find out that working at home in their own businesses gave them enormous freedom and didn't diminish human contact at all. They could dress as they pleased when they were not seeing clients and work during whatever part of the day suited them. They were in constant telephone contact with at least as many people as they were accustomed to contacting in a corporate setting.

THE WRONG, WRONG ANSWER

But still, you might ask, how can one small experiment be at all useful in the face of the overwhelming global problems we face? Whenever I think of how change occurs, I go back in my memory to teaching high school sociology. My class studied group process by engaging in a series of experiments. In one of these I would privately pick the student with the greatest ego strength as a guinea pig and send that student out of the room on a short errand while I explained to the rest of the class how the experiment would work and asked for volunteers.

When the guinea-pig student returned, I made a pretense of selecting five students at random—the student who had left the room, and the four others who had already volunteered. I lined up the five students so that the student who was the guinea pig would be fourth in line. Then I showed all five students three bars on a chart and asked each one in turn to say which bar was the same height as a bar on another chart. The four students who had volunteered were coached in advance to give a particular wrong answer in each round. The guinea-pig student, then, would hear three students give identical wrong answers before having a chance to respond, and then he or she would be followed by one more student giving the same wrong answer. As the rounds progressed, would the guinea-pig student begin to question his or her own judgment in the face of so much agreement between the others?

This was by far the most interesting and revealing experiment we did all year, at least as much for the guinea-pig student as for the rest of us. It is very hard to hold your point of view when the whole world goes against you, and, more often than not, the student would cave in and go along with the others by the third or fourth round.

But in the course of doing this experiment I discovered another piece of data that I had not anticipated. Invariably one of the students who volunteered would decide that the experiment would be more realistic if one student gave a wrong answer *different* from the wrong answer given by the other students in the experiment. When this happened, it dramatically altered the outcome, because that one crack in unanimity gave the guinea-pig student new confidence. If even one other person saw things differently from the mass—even if it was still the wrong answer—there was a chance that he or she might be right after all.

AWAKENING CONSTRUCTIVE DOUBT

I have thought of these experiments over the years and have noticed how the patterns I learned from them still work in my own life. It is terribly difficult to hold my own perspective when the whole world, like a monolith, sees things in one particular other way, but not so hard if there is even one other point of view. As an adult, for example, you can have more influence in the life of a child than you realize by saying what you believe to be true if it is out of step with the norm. The child may not come around to where you stand, but your view may be just what is needed to help the child hold onto his or her own emerging view. That may be the reason why a particular coach or teacher is able to have such a disproportionate impact on the life of an individual student.

When I lived in suburbia, I experienced a monolithic worldview about lifestyle. I found it very difficult to hold onto my own idea that I might enjoy living a much simpler life, because there was so much agreement in the culture about what was essential for good living. Deep in the unconscious assumptions of our urban/suburban culture, *simpler really means poorer*, no matter how we might argue otherwise. I think this is why we can know that our planet is in trouble and still not be able to stop using up its resources. The unanimity about what is a desirable standard of living is so great that, like the guinea-pig student, most of us cannot hold onto any other perception of reality without a great deal of effort.

Moving to the country has served as that one crack in social unanimity that has allowed me to really think differently about my lifestyle. This experience has illustrated for me how our ability to be affected by even one other disparate point of view might help us to change our minds, bit by bit, as Harman describes, so that major change can eventually occur. I was able to change my mind about my lifestyle because I am now living in the midst of people who do not pay much attention to the part of urban/suburban life that was most deadening for me: malls and entertainment complexes, three-lane highways and all-night streetlights, and high-fashion clothing. There is far less pressure to continually upgrade one's home or to get degrees or other credentials to advance one's future. It is not that people in the country never think of these things, but that these things all take a distant second to the pleasure of being outside in a natural environment on a regular basis.

So instead of making a costly foray into ski country for a weekend, for example, country people might go snowshoeing, cross-country skiing, or snowmobiling after a fresh snow over hills and through woods that are owned by someone they probably know, with few fences or warnings to the trespasser. Or in my case, there are the endless hours I spend shoveling the snow off my pond's imperfect ice, getting my sustenance as much from the view around me and the exhilaration of the sun and wind as from the skating itself.

There is a new perspective with every season. Walking to the top of my hill in summer and looking out over the horizon, I can sense how solid the earth is, like an old and eternally loyal friend. Down below, the water in the brook and its tributaries rhythmically rolls along to the White River and eventually to the ocean. It all fits together. The whole system moves and changes, but in its own time and in its own way. The natural setting is communicating to me something that is counter to what I thought I knew about how to live. This land, like my country neighbors, has penetrated my consciousness. Like that one student in my experiment who chose the wrong, wrong answer, my new environment has awakened doubt.

Awakened doubt can nudge us toward the creative experimentation that can result in our changing our minds in the small ways that eventually add up to major change. Living in rural America, for example, opened up my thinking about the house in which I live. When I came here, I bought a house that looked pretty normal by suburban Boston standards. I did all the conventionally right things. I paid enough for my new house to avoid paying capital gains tax on the profits from my old one, and I got twenty-one gorgeous acres in the bargain. I examined the resale potential of the house and decided it was good. When I began living here, however, I discovered how cozy and livable, and inexpensive, a house can be. I understand now about the utility of mudrooms, and I think about arranging my house so that people arriving in boots and with dogs will feel really welcome. I began to allow myself to consider that a formal living room is really superfluous for me. I hardly ever use the one I have. What I think about now is how I want my space to work, not what my house *should* have and what will enhance its resale value.

The best news is that the most important contribution to my thinking about simplifying my living space came not from the stick of potential catastrophe, but from the carrot of amazing creativity. There are many homes in this area that I like a great deal more than my own, and they all cost a lot less than I am paying. Seeing what else is possible has freed me from suburban standards. In a new mood of architectural independence, my husband and I marked out on the back lawn a potential design for our next house. It is about 60 percent of the size of our current house, probably still larger than we need. We brought chairs out and sat in the rooms to see how they would feel. We drive around now, thinking about what the right land would be—a westerly view, a brook and/or a pond, and a sunny meadow for my gardens. Within the next several years, I predict, we will find our way into a much smaller home of our own design.

My experience of rethinking my house is a good example of the impact that even one other disparate view can have in helping us to adapt ourselves to the needs of the future faster than we think we can. If we can trust our instincts and let go of being visible in the conventional world, we can build new businesses and redesign existing businesses so that they can have the same kind of impact—that is, they can help us to adapt ourselves to the future faster than we think we can. I feel strongly that some of the coming change will be painful, for the earth may not be able to wait for us to figure out that our current lifestyle is too rich for its blood. But it is enormously encouraging to see that, one by one, we may choose change on our own by seeing what other people are doing that goes against the current. There is real pleasure in discovering that we have, all along, had some good ideas of our own about how to live and work. And that small experiments, in which every one of us is capable of engaging, have the potential to produce fundamental change on a much larger scale.

LIVING LIGHTLY

The fact that outdoor life in the country is so rich that I need and want less in terms of indoor space—even in a place where winter lasts six months of the year—led me to a major discovery, one that I have known conceptually for a long time, but have never been able to integrate into my life: I can live on far less money than I assumed I could. Needing less money, in turn, gives me more flexibility in my business. I can take the time to contemplate what I *could* be doing rather than what needs to be done right now to generate a certain level of revenue. Needing less money also means that, if I wish, I can spend less time producing for my business and more time engaged in my community. I am not advocating a policy of scarcity, but a policy of flexibility—the less I *must* have or think I *should* have, the more power I have to decide what I really want to do in my life, and the more chance I have to contribute something of lasting value.

Even when hard financial realities force people to accept a change in lifestyle, the end results can sometimes be more a blessing than a curse. I have discovered this in my own life, and I know I am not alone. A new word is finding its way into newspaper and magazine articles: "downshifting." It is a trend among more and more people who are finding mainstream middle-class economic life too stressful and unfulfilling and are actively choosing alternatives. In contrast to the ethic of upward mobility, they are consciously accepting less financial reward so that they can have more time for themselves and for their families. If we are lucky, these people will be able to share their realizations and experiences and help us all to redefine what it means to have a quality life.

It is also interesting to note that in difficult economic times, the formation of new businesses actually increases. If people are laid off and cannot find a job replacement, starting their own businesses may be their only alternative. From such experiences of personal crises can come our greatest innovations.

Especially in times of change, a critical aspect of feminine leadership, I believe, is keeping the feminine contextual questions ever present in our minds. What is really happening historically and what is *life* asking of me as a result? And what is life asking of us as a society as a whole? If we put these questions first, at some point our increased awareness will require that we subordinate financial and lifestyle goals to goals and purposes that are more aligned with the needs of the whole—our whole psyches, our whole community, our whole global family. The trouble for me, and I suspect for others, is that while I thought I had subordinated financial security to a higher regard for life, I only got a glimpse of what that could mean when I had been tested, even in a small way, by only one unusually unstable period in my business. I am part of a generation and a class that has never experienced real economic depression. Nor have I ever lived in a country where war has been raging outside my door or where an epidemic has taken thousands of lives. It is all too easy to continue to live in the illusion that my life will always move forward in a positive direction—as if I could go on accumulating more knowledge and skill and money, like a snowball rolling down a hill. The ease of my life to-date leaves me ill-prepared for what I might be called upon to cope with, if history is any indication of what is possible.

Creating personal financial flexibility through deliberately living below one's means may be the soundest strategy for our turbulent times. I do not want to belabor this point, or ignore the real hardships that many families in this country are facing as profits increase and real wages decrease, but at some point, I feel, we have to tell ourselves the truth about the excesses of our consumer economy. And when we think about it, is it realistic to ask ourselves and our partners to be less driven in our busi- nesses, if we insist on aspiring to ever more complex material lifestyles? Such drivenness doesn't seem to work for our psyches any more than it does for the world as a whole, and it certainly does not leave us any time for the inner work that we need to do to find our real passion.

We have made up endless rules for ourselves about finan- cial credibility: home ownership in a neighborhood with a cer- tain status, sending our children to certain schools and colleges, appropriate amounts of time spent in one job at a certain level before moving on, appropriate career moves, how much to sock away in an IRA or pension plan before retirement, and so on, and so forth. These rules are not without some wisdom, but it is amazing how completely we take these things for granted.

Feminine leadership means going beyond the conventional wisdom and finding the deep passion within which we can make our action in the world spontaneous and uniquely our own. When a person finds his or her inner passion and purpose and subordinates the practical aspects of career development and financial success to the call from within, the pattern of that person's life may or may not look all that different, but the driving force will have changed, as the following stories illustrate.

INSPIRATIONS FROM THE FIELD

Hollie Shaner is a registered nurse and has worked in all kinds of clinical settings since she graduated in 1976. Originally from Hollywood, Florida, and a long-time beach lover, she was on vacation in York, Maine, on the beach with her children at dawn. She felt something hitting her ankle in the water and felt around until she found a foam soda can cover that said "HOLLYWOOD, FLORIDA." It hit her just how far that piece of waste had traveled, one piece of many that cluttered that beautiful beach. She found herself with tears in her eyes wondering what it would be like in twenty years. It was a moment of truth, she said, a message from the universe.

Hollie went home to Vermont and started to recycle. She and her family got serious about reducing waste by changing how they purchased things and by composting, but then, she said, she would go off to work at Fletcher Allen Hospital in Burlington and create more and different waste. When she asked the hospital administrators and staff why they did not recycle, the answer was that they were not required to. So she told them about Vermont's Act 78, which mandates the reduction of solid waste in the state by 40 percent by the year 2000. To do its share, she told them, the hospital would have to reduce its solid waste by over one ton per day!

If I ever had cause to doubt my own premise that each person has her own unique nature and gifts, that doubt would have been put to rest by my conversation with Hollie Shaner. She has an encyclopedic grasp of environmental details that I cannot begin to fathom. She did extensive research on hospital waste and found that the only information available covered infectious waste, which is what we assume hospital waste is all about. Together with her colleague, Connie Leach-Bisson, who operated the ReStore in Burlington, she spent six months setting up a research grant proposal called MedCycle™ Study, which was funded by the Vermont Department of Natural Resources. For a thirty-day period they collected the waste from 982 surgical procedures—all of which was generated *before* the surgical procedures began.

Then, from June to September, they spent at least two days a week in the basement of Fletcher Allen Hospital sorting the contents. They found that 34 percent of the waste was sterilization wrappers, the vast majority of which were unlabeled so they could not be recycled. They did not even need to use surgical gloves to sort the trash, thus debunking the myth that all waste coming out of surgery is contaminated.

After months of volunteer labor, Hollie wrote herself a job description and became the hospital's waste manager. But that was just the beginning. She later reduced her hours at the hospital and, with her partner Glen McRae, formed CGH Environmental Strategies in 1991 to consult to hospitals, doing waste audits and helping hospital staffs develop baseline data so they can measure their progress in waste reduction. She likes to teach hospital organizations how to become self-sufficient in managing solid waste programs. In addition her company helps those same manufacturers whose waste she had analyzed as part of her study, produce more environmentally sound packaging. Together Hollie and her partner have published three books on waste management in health care through the American Hospital Association (*An Ounce of Prevention, Waste Management in Merger Conditions: Optimizing Systems,* and *A Guidebook for Hospital Waste Management*). These books are full of stories from the many people who called Holly when her program in Burlington began to attract attention.

Hollie doesn't seem to need much sleep. In addition to her business and her management job at the hospital, she also got her master's degree in 1995. But with two teenagers at home, she began to restrict her business trips to no more than twice a month in early 1996. Holly is not a woman who wants to build an empire, but a woman who got inspired about solving a problem and gave her considerable talents to that effort.

Deborah Barlow was a working artist in New York City for ten years before she married, moved to a suburb of Boston, had three kids in three years, and started a business with her husband. She calls this intense period of her life "boot camp squared." In 1986 at age thirty-five, when Lotus Development Corporation acquired her product, she moved on to the position of vice president of marketing of a $50 million high-tech company with thirty-five people working directly for her. She loved the "wild ride" of the hot PC industry, but she found herself drawn to taking courses in the spiritual dimension. "What is this all about?" she began to ask about her work. "Is this all there is?" By 1991 the answer was clear: "not for me." After four years of searching for meaning, she decided she could not find what she was looking for in a corporate environment.

Today Deborah goes to her art studio from 7 A.M. to 2 P.M. In the afternoon she conducts what she calls the "other parts of my life"—consulting and developing business strategies for companies, being a mom to three teenagers, and serving on a few select nonprofit boards. She "cleared the deck" of all the other "do-gooder" work she had been doing.

Her passion now is painting, something that she says never left her body. Her first mission is creating art that heals, art that connects the viewer with the sacredness of the object, art that can shift the energy in a human being. She hopes her art will never be able to be reproduced on the Internet or in a photograph, because the intent of her art is to evoke in the viewer a state that is calm, peaceful, and authentic. For her art to do its work, there needs to be a real connection between the viewer and the texture of the original artwork itself.

Like primitive art, her work is designed to evoke awe and a sense of spiritual power. She reveres the relationship between the tangible and the intangible and has complete faith in the diffuse awareness of her audience to take in the meaning of her art. Her work is an example of the feminine affirmation of life. This principle is usually so muted in businesspeople but it permeates her entire conversation.

Her second mission is to create "unexpected environments," not only for her own work but for other artists as well. A gallery, she says, is not the best place to see art, certainly not the place where the general public will see it. In addition to selling her art directly out of her studio, she had three major shows last year, all of them in alternative spaces, including the Boston Police Department. At first, the police officers and other workers in the building were openly disdainful: what did these pictures have to do with police work? But over time their attitudes changed. Now people who work in that building have become very involved with her process. Now they want to go with her to her studio and pick out what will be hung next. While she would never say that her artwork is not for sale, her work is audience driven. "People in forgotten, unexpected environments do care," she says, and those are the audiences she wants to reach. She is exploring the idea of similar rotating exhibitions in business settings.

Deborah has been out of full-time work in the corporate world for four years now. She continues to consult in that world, but when she sees her old colleagues socially in the role of artist, she sometimes feels invisible. She says she had forgotten how little value the world attaches to artists, and she was shocked at first to find out how much she missed the positional power of being a vice president. She still values what she learned in business, and she uses those skills, especially marketing, daily. But she has "deconstructed" caring about upward mobility and security. That is what happens, she says, when you turn your life over to something else. She is aware of the buffer that her substantial salary created for her, and the texture of her life has now changed. She lives in the same house she lived in twelve years ago; while she is conscious that other people she knows have moved on to larger homes. She used to have full-time help; now she teaches her kids to pitch in. There used to be more time and money for vacations, but none of this seems to be important to her now.

When you talk to Deborah, what you notice most is her energy. My pen could not keep up with the excitement and pleasure that flowed with her words into the telephone. Her commitment to her audience and to creating new environments for artists is palpable and contagious. Her work is an example of an experiment that could have far-reaching effects—on the way art affects our work lives and on the accessibility of art to the public. Deborah is a pocket of energy creating a new form.

In 1987 *Sandy Cohen* was a successful commercial real estate broker in Dallas, Texas. She was in her late forties, feeling unhappy and unhealthy, and wondering how to find out who she really was. She had rejected her Jewish heritage earlier in her life, but in this troublesome time, she went back to it. She joined the Israeli Army Program, which pushed her to her limits and started her asking herself what she was "here" for. She had always been a follower of Gandhi, so from Israel she went to India. With her daughter she crisscrossed the country and then went on to a worldwide odyssey that included almost all the continents.

When Sandy went abroad she found a real connection with values that had been important to her from childhood. She did not visit cities, but villages. She found whole villages that were like families, where people really meant it when they called each other brother and sister. In such communities all over the world she experienced—perhaps for the first time—a sense of being really cared for by an entire group. In America, she says, we are so self-centered. We have a lifestyle that separates. The thicker the walls of our homes, the more separate we are.

As she listened to a conversation in Bombay between two women by the side of the road, she came to understand how little she needed an expensive habitat to be safe and part of the human family. What existed between those two women and in all the villages she visited was, she realized, "undestroyable." And I understand completely what she meant. What Sandy tapped into was what I have called deep community. What she hungered for and found was a communal experience of sacred regard.

I first met Sandy at a conference in March of 1993 in Dallas. She invited a large group of us to her home on Saturday night. We knew that Sandy had started a company called Global Family, but we had no idea that her home was also her warehouse. When we got there, we found ourselves in the midst of the most exquisite merchandise. Though it was not her intention, Sandy, who had just returned from a trip to South America, sold a lot of merchandise that night. She had not even priced items yet, and had to call an associate to get that information, because we were relentless. I came home to Vermont with a Peruvian necklace of blue lapis stone in fine silver work that is now my most precious piece of jewelry.

Through Global Family Sandy traveled the world negotiating with people in those small villages. She bought their crafts at a fair price and brought them back to the United States. She did not sell merchandise to retail outlets unless those outlets were willing to display the merchandise such that each piece could tell its own story: how and where it was made and who its creator/author was. Over time she found that such displays were much easier to do in museums, so she had already started to develop museums as distribution points when another opportunity presented itself.

In 1991 an organization was founded in Dallas called HOPE—Honoring of People Everywhere—to bring the diverse groups in Dallas together in a mutually respectful way. In five years' time, HOPE had developed programs in fifty elementary schools, which bore signs that read WE ARE A HOPE SCHOOL. The kids, she says, get totally caught up in learning about each other. During the time of the bombing in Oklahoma City, HOPE facilitated a meeting when a Pakistani in the community had said, "I am not a terrorist. I just want to be a part of Dallas life." The emotions at that meeting went from wildly angry to tears of compassion; at the meeting's end even the angriest people asked if they could participate. In March of 1995 during the mayoral election, an Iranian man told Sandy that he didn't understand much about the election. This sparked an idea in her that resulted in a HOPE reception for mayoral candidates hosted by people in the Dallas community from fifty countries.

Sandy is the catalyst in HOPE, the person who creates the space for things to happen. Soon she found that she had to choose between her work in HOPE and traveling for Global Family. In 1993 she chose HOPE, because she felt her energy was needed there, and she wanted to create a model program including the television programming that had emerged. Not being afraid to re-sort old seeds in a new configuration, as many people on a conventionally upwardly mobile path might have been, Sandy went back into real estate to make financial ends meet.

As I listened to Sandy, I could see that what she is trying to do is replicate in Dallas what she found in global villages. People do not have a frame of reference for this, she says. Recently someone asked, "How can I support it?" "Don't support it," she replied. "Understand it." Sandy is using everything she has learned—from teaching, running businesses, politics, and travel—to bring deep community into people's consciousness. It takes the experience of both worlds—spiritual and political—to do this kind of work, she says. It is not a question of "either-or."

Sandy puts her soul into her work as much as Deborah and Hollie do. This is the calling from within that cannot be denied.

When HOPE started, Sandy found herself letting go of long-term goals. Now she just goes inside and asks herself, "Am I on the right track?" On the right track means being in tune with life, in tune with herself. Like Hollie and Deborah, Sandy's energy over-flows, probably one of the most telling signs that one is on one's true path.

Each one of these women has connected with her individual nature and is doing work that she feels called to do. Each is using her considerable worldly skills to manifest an internal vision. Like that third-place driver who advanced to first at Thunder Road, each woman saw the chance to take the lead in her own domain and took it—consciously. The really good news within all these stories is that leadership can take many forms. There are opportunities for everyone. The small uncharted experiments may be as productive for the long term—and as challenging—as the visible acts of power wielded in high places. We are not all going to be president of Microsoft, but we don't need to be to make a real difference.

SUMMING UP

Feminine leadership has very little to do, in my mind, with positions or conventional power. It has to do with what sub-stance we bring into the world from our own central core. To tap into this energy, we have to know who we are, and that takes painstaking inner work. We also have to know who we are not, and that takes a willingness to value and collaborate with the "other." Finally we have to be willing to do work we are called to do, however different that work may turn out to be from the career that we had in mind. But the rewards are immense, and the excitement and challenge are as adrenaline producing as taking the lead in a stock-car race when there is nothing in front of you but an open track.

Chapter 13

Conclusion

The open racetrack is a good metaphor for where we are today. Our political and economic worlds are changing rapidly. Our job is to get as skilled as possible at observing what is real. That means observing how all the changes and the constant elements of life are related to each other. Only then can we make good long-term decisions about when to make the turns of life and at what pace. The truth is that there is not much out in front for any of us to follow. We cannot even look to the megacorporations that were such clear-cut leaders only a short time ago.

Illuminating the qualities of the feminine principle, in the hope that it can help us with the task in front of us, has been the main purpose of this book. At the heart of the matter, I believe, the feminine principle is concerned about relationship. I hesitate to use that word, because our thinking about relationship can be so simplistic. Relationship means a lot more than just getting along with other people. Relationship exists in nonhuman and even nonliving domains, right down to atomic and subatomic particles. All of nature and spirit are intertwined, and life is beautiful and terrible at the same time. We cannot reduce the feminine concern for relationship simply to something that is nice. Every relationship within our universe requires our careful observation, our respect, and even our awe.

It seems entirely fitting, therefore, as I finish this book on a snowy Saturday in March, that, like many other people in my community, I am interrupting myself to make stew for Town Meeting Dinner next week. Still others are attending a funeral. Together as a community we are engaged in the working relationships of life, preparing food and grieving our losses. Next Tuesday we will take one full day out of our regular schedules for Town Meeting to elect officers, haggle over budget issues, and break bread together. The grand finale will be the homemade pies for which Tunbridge kitchens are famous.

As more of us experiment with new patterns in business, I believe, we will find that these ordinary experiences of living will be more a part of our day-to-day work lives. We will be trying to learn how to recognize and honor good working relationships—with our fellow workers, with our products, with our clients and colleagues, and with the earth itself. Cumulatively we can build a new set of *standards* about relationship in our public life that are as sophisticated as our extraordinary standards in focused consciousness thinking.

These new standards will require that we learn sacred regard, that we become conscious of and respect the subjective reality of others, and that we integrate this understanding into our perceptions of the world as a whole. Our brains are so facile at focused consciousness thinking that we are repeatedly caught in the trap of missing inner essence altogether and believing that only what we consider to be objectively right matters. This view results in all kinds of problems at the microlevel; the effects can easily be seen in the local political conflicts in any small town. These small-town problems are paralleled by similar problems at the macro level, where we are not yet able to take in enough information to identify with the whole global system. From one end of the spectrum to the other, what is missing is a deep understanding about relationship. This is the heart of what Sandy Cohen is working on in Dallas.

I refuse to consider our difficulties with relationship as a natural, and inevitable, human shortcoming. This attitude seems to me to be a failure on our part to imagine what is possible. When John F. Kennedy announced that we would get to the moon before the end of a decade, we assumed that we could learn what we needed to know in order to do it. I believe we can do the same in the arena of relationship. In order to develop the systems that will satisfy the earth's requirements for sustainability and our human hunger for peace, we need to strengthen diffuse awareness, practice the affirmation of life that is expressed by presence and being, accept the cycles of life, and cultivate the sacred regard of deep community. We will also need to feel deeply, trust radically, mother ourselves and our coworkers so that our unique potentials can be brought forth, and become more attuned to the spaces within which we work.

Learning to use these feminine attitudes and skills, in collaboration with masculine focused consciousness, to develop new human standards for relationship in all our public institutions is, in my mind, the great challenge of our time. My yearning to illuminate the feminine principle, and my belief that a new collaboration between masculine and feminine energy is possible in the public sphere, became really conscious to me when I had the following dream. It was *the* dream that made me take my dreams seriously. I dreamt that a black woman and her son were living in my apartment but hadn't paid back rent, and I was leaving that apartment because I didn't think I could make ends meet. Then, in another scene, I was floating in a pool of water and drifting toward a very long waterfall. I plunged over the falls fully expecting to crash on the rocks below, but my body, of its own accord, realigned itself into a dive position. (I know nothing about how to do this in real life.) I then dove into a very deep pool and came to the surface, exhilarated, and somewhat incredulously shouting, "I made it!" My husband, who was also in the pool, laughed that sheepish way you do when you have just escaped a harrowing fate by inches. When I started to dive again, the water disappeared, and there was a reddish purple marble floor of a cathedral. I just walked down to the back of the cathedral where a celebration was in process. My husband Bob turned to me and said, "I love you."

I woke up in one of those afterglows that occurs when the unconscious has reached through to you and left you with an image that is profoundly comforting and encouraging. I have carried that feeling of the dive with me ever since. But I was confused by the meaning of the black woman, even though I am aware of Marion Woodman's work on the Black Madonna, which she sees as an image of the instinctual feminine (Woodman 1990). So I did some "active imagination" with the black woman about our relationship and her rent payment. Active imagination is a process of meditating on the dream figure and asking it questions while you are awake. I sat for a full five minutes before this woman chose to talk to me, but then she told me that I didn't really have to take care of her and her son. The gist of her message was for me to stop struggling so hard to make sure that everything in my practical, external life worked perfectly. I did not need to make so many focused consciousness connections all the time, she advised. "Didn't I know what to do when I dove off the precipice? Actually," she said, as she smiled at her son, "*we* knew what to do."

I believe we can bring the masculine and feminine energy together in our public life in a new pattern that will exponentially increase our options for the future. I believe that there is something very basic inside us, a capacity that the woman of my dream and her son represents, that can bring the best of both feminine and masculine together, if we are willing to be guided from within and if we are willing to take the dive.

References

Barreno, Maria, et al. 1975. *The New Portuguese Letters, The Three Marias.* Great Britain: Paladin.

Berry, Wendell. 1975. *The Memory of Old Jack.* New York: Harcourt Brace, Jovanovich.

———. 1982. *A Place on Earth.* Rev. ed. San Francisco: North Point Press.

Blum, Robert. 1982. *The Book of Runes.* New York: St. Martin's Press.

Bly, Robert, and Marion Woodman. 1992. *On Men and Women.* Canada: Applewood Communications. Six-part video.

Brittain, Vera. 1940. *Testament of Friendship.* New York: Seaview Books.

Claremont de Castillejo, Irene. 1973. *Knowing Woman: A Feminine Psychology.* Harper Colophon Books.

From D Day to the Rhine with Bill Moyers. 1994. Narr. Bill Moyers. PBS. June 5.

DePree, Max. 1987. *Leadership Is an Art.* East Lansing, Mich.: Michigan State University Press.

Fox, Matthew. 1983a. *Meditations with Meister Eckhart.* Santa Fe: Bear & Co.

———. 1983b. *Original Blessing: A Primer in Creation Spirituality.* Santa Fe: Bear & Co.

———. 1995. *The Reinvention of Work: A New Vision of Livelihood for Our Time.* San Francisco: Harper.

Franz, Marie Louise von. 1972. *The Feminine in Fairy Tales*. Dallas: Spring Publications; rev. ed., Boston: Shambhala, 1993.

Gilligan, Carol. 1993. *In a Different Voice: Psychological Theory and Women's Development*. Cambridge, Mass.: Harvard University Press.

Gozdz, Kazimierz. 1995. *Community Building: Renewing Spirit and Learning*. San Francisco: New Leaders Press.

Grafton, Sue. 1995. *K Is for Killer*. New York: Fawcett.

Griffin, W. E. B. 1987–89. Brotherhood of War Series. Vols 1–8. New York: Jove Publications.

Hall, Nor. 1994. *The Moon and the Virgin*. New York: Harper Collins.

Hannah, Barbara. 1981. *Encounters with the Soul: Active Imagination as Developed by C. G. Jung*. Boston: Sigo Press.

———. 1987. *Striving Toward Wholeness*. Boston: Sigo Press.

Harding, Esther. 1990. *The Way of All Woman*. Boston: Shambhala.

Harman, Willis. 1991. *Global Mind Change: The Promise of the Last Years of the Twentieth Century*. Boston: Sigo Press.

Hawken, Paul. 1993. *The Ecology of Commerce*. New York: Harper Business.

Jordan, Judith V., et al. 1991. *Women's Growth in Connection: Writings from the Stone Center*. New York: Guilford Press.

Jung, C. G. 1971. *Psychological Types. Collected Works of C. G. Jung*, vol. 6. Bollingen Series, No. 20. Princeton, N.J.: Princeton University Press.

———. 1973. *Memories, Dreams and Reflections*. Ed. Aneila Jaffe. New York: Pantheon Books.

Keen, Sam. 1987. "Men, Women and War." *Creation Magazine* (May/June).

Kubler-Ross, Elisabeth. 1991. *On Death and Dying*. New York: Macmillan.

Lonergan, Anne, and Caroline Richards, ed. 1987. *Thomas Berry and the New Cosmology*. Mystic, Conn.: Twenty-Third Publications.

McCaulley, Mary H. 1994. "Types and Gender." *Bulletin of Psychological Type* 17, no. 1: 15–16.

Miles, Margaret. 1990. "Women's Desire and Personal Change." Theological Opportunities Program Lecture, Harvard University Divinity School, Cambridge, Mass., September 27.

Monick, Eugene. 1987. *Phallos: Sacred Images of the Masculine*. Toronto: Inner City Books.

Moore, Thomas. 1994. *Care of the Soul: A Guide for Cultivating Depth and Sacredness in Everyday Life*. New York: Harper Collins.

Muller, Robert. 1978. *But Most of All They Taught Me Happiness*. Garden City, N.Y.: Image Books.

Munk, Nina. 1995. "The Best Man for the Job Is Your Wife." *Forbes*, November 20, 148–54.

NE Thing Enterprises. 1993. *Magic Eye*. New York: Scholastic.

Neumann, Erich. 1990. *Amor and Psyche: The Psychic Development of the Feminine*. Bollingen Series 54. Princeton, N.J.: Princeton University Press.

O'Toole, Patricia. 1990. "Thrifty, Kind—and Smart as Hell." *Lear's*, October.

Peck, M. Scott. 1985. *The Road Less Traveled*. New York: Simon & Schuster.

———. 1987. *The Different Drum: Community Making and Peace*. New York: Simon & Schuster.

Peters, Tom. 1987. *Thriving on Chaos: Handbook for a Management Revolution*. New York: Alfred A. Knopf.

Qualls-Corbett, Nancy. 1988. *The Sacred Prostitute*. Toronto: Inner City Books.

Quinn, Daniel. 1993. *Ishmael*. New York: Bantam Books.

Scrimgeour, G. J. 1982. *A Woman of Her Times*. New York, G. P. Putnam's Sons.

Stein, Murray. 1988. *In Midlife*. Dallas: Spring Publications.

Stein, Robert. 1988. *Incest and Human Love: The Betrayal of Soul in Psychotherapy*. Dallas: Spring Publications.

Swimme, Brian. 1984. *The Universe Is a Green Dragon: A Cosmic Creation Story*. Santa Fe: Bear & Co.

Swimme, Brian, and Matthew Fox. 1987. *Four Great Revelations of Ancient Religion and the New Science*. Oakland: Friends of Creation Spirituality. Two-part videotape.

U. S. Department of Agriculture. 1961. *SEEDS: The Yearbook of Agriculture, 1961*. Washington, D.C.: U.S. Government Printing Office.

Wharton, Edith. 1985. *Novels: The House of Mirth, The Reef, The Custom of the Country, The Age of Innocence*. New York: Literary Classics of America.

Whitmont, Edward C. 1984. *Return of the Goddess*. New York: The Crossroad Publishing Co.

Woodman, Marion. 1982. *Addiction to Perfection: The Still Unravished Bride.* Toronto: Inner City Books.

———. 1985. *The Pregnant Virgin.* Toronto: Inner City Books.

———. 1990. *Rolling Away the Stone.* Boulder, Colo.: Sounds True Recording. Audiotape.

Zukav, Gary. 1984. *The Dancing Wu Li Masters: An Overview of the New Physics.* New York: Bantam New Age Books.

Index

A

A Guidebook for Hospital Waste Management (American Hospital Association), 190
A Place on Earth (Berry), 66–67
A Woman of Her Times (Scrimgeour), 96
Acceptance of self, 42
Action, organizing, 81–94
Active imagination, 200
Administrators, identification with top, 165–66
Affirming life, 31–43
Age of Peace and Freedom, 86
Age of Plenty, 86
Ambience of comfort level, 21
Ambrose, Stephen, 101
America, living in rural, 184
American Hospital Association, 190
An Ounce of Prevention (American Hospital Association), 190
Anderson, Susan, 4
Anger, ego-based, 124
Anima woman, 163, 169
Answer, wrong, wrong, 181–82
Aphrodite, 4
Apollo, 36
Appreciation, feeling of spontaneous, 68
Archetypal feminine, xiv, 8
Athena, 47–48
Atkins, Linda, 117
Augustine, St., 37–39, 93
Authentic values
  and deep community, 74
  of persons, 73

Authenticity, 104
Autonomy in business, 54
Awareness
  diffuse, xv, 15–29
  source of one's, 136

B

Babilonia, Tai, 167–68
Balance, maintaining, 168–69
Barlow, Deborah, 190–92
Bart, Lily, 95
Beauty, simple natural, 42–43
Berry, Wendell, 10, 66–67, 127
Beyond War movement, 106–8
Birth, giving, 46–49
Black Madonna, 200
Blizzard of '78 (Boston), 62, 70
Bly, Robert, 31, 40, 170
Boat float, 129
Boot camp squared, 190
Borei, Jeanne, 62
Both-and and either-or mind-sets, 23–26
Bradbury, Ray, 58
Briggs, Katherine, 110
Brittain, Vera, 87
Business
  autonomy in, 54
  contractual, 70
  culture, 69
  and deep community, 71–76
  diffuse awareness as asset, 26–29
  formation of new, 186
  transition house for, 99

Business (*continued*)
  upheavals, 98
  using good judgment, 50
Businesspeople, working with, 22
Businesspeople's Anonymous, 99–100

C

Care of the Soul (Moore), 113
CGH Environmental Strategies, 189
Change
  patterns of, 179–95
  times of, 88–93
Child, loving a, 116
Choreography, masculine/feminine, 167–70
Christmas Eve and the solstice, 58
Claremont de Castillejo, Irene, xv, 5, 15, 61, 67
Clinton, Bill, 99
Cohen, Sandy, 192–95, 198
Collectivity, new understanding of, 93–94
Communities
  absence of, 64
  discomfort with, 67–71
  electronic, 68
  embracing, 73
  and indifference, 64
  invisible, 69
  sense of, 42–43
Community, deep, xv, 61–77, 193
Companion planting, 17–18
Comradeship, wartime, 72
Conception, dynamics of, 170–73
Confessions (St. Augustine), 37, 93
Conflicts, multiple, 165
Consciousness
  connections, 154
  feminine, 154, 179–80
  focused, 5–6, 15, 27, 36, 87
  masculine, 10
  new, 154–56
  problems of, 156
Consensus building and dialog, 21
Container and orchestrator, 173–74
Contractual business, 70
CRA Managed Care, Inc. (Boston), 136–38
Creation Magazine, 2
Creation, spontaneous, 166–67
Creative Change Technologies, 62
Culture, urban/suburban, 183
Cycles of life, accepting the, 45–59

D

D day, 100–101

Dark
  awareness of the, 57
  and light relationship, 58
  loving the, 56–59
Darrow, George, 176
Data management, whole picture of, 22–23
Daughter, Miller's, 148–54
Death and dying, 49–51
Deep community, xv, 61–77, 193
  and authentic values, 74
  foundation level for our lives, 62
  importance of business in, 71–76
  increasing self-esteem, 74–75
  wartime comradeship, 72
DePree, Max, 139–40
Depth psychology, Jungian, xii, 96
Desire, female, 37–38
Despair and the love of night, 58–59
Detachment, 39
Development, moral, 41–42
Diffuse awareness, xv, 15–29
  as a business asset, 26–29
  defined, 16
  extraordinary potential tool, 29
  and feelings of aliveness, 20
  feminine, 17
  and intuition, 23
  using at work, 20–23
Dionysus, 36
Disconnection and reconnection, 64–67
Diverging and converging, 9–11
Doubt, awakening constructive, 182–85
Downshifting, 186
Dysfunctional families, 104

E

Earth
  love of, 177
  saving the, 159–61
Eckhart, Meister, 62
Ecology of Commerce, The (Hawken), 11
Economic life
  new frame for, 55
  what's missing, 6–9
Ego-based anger, 124
Eisenhower, Dwight D., 100–101
Elder, Irma, 88
Electronic communities, 68
Emotions, controlling, 96
EMT (emergency medical technician), 66
Energy
  containing and orchestrating human, 173

masculine, 17, 172–73
masculine and feminine, 161
Entrophy defined, 98
Eros, Psyche's encounter with, 175–76
Essex Conference Center (Massachusetts),
132–33
Evolution, 52–53
Experimentation, slow and deliberate,
85

F

Failure, cycles of, 53
Fairness
feminine sense of, 40
public world of men, 40
Families, dysfunctional, 104
Fathering, affirming accomplishments,
117
Fear, 64–65, 160–61
from the unknown, 156
Feelings
deep, 95–111
function, 109–10
giving value to what is thought, 106
of sacred regard, 68
as values, 105–11
Female
moral development stages, 41–42
nature of desire, 37–38
Feminine; *See also* Masculine; Women
affirmation of life, 32, 43
archetypal, xiv, 8
consciousness, 154, 179–80
as container and orchestrator, 173–74
depths, 145–61
energy, 161
essence, 153
leadership, 161, 178
life principle, 172
as lover, 175–78
passion, 37–39, 161
principle, 146, 197
rage, 119–25
Feminine in Fairy Tales, The (von Franz),
148–50
Finances
credibility, 187–88
security, 187
Focused consciousness, 5–6, 15, 27, 87
Forbes magazine, 88
Fox, Matthew, 10
Franz, Marie Louise von. *See* von Franz
Freedom, age of, 86
Freeman, Orville, 86
Future, adapting to the, 185

G

Garden
the, 17–20
working in one's own, 147–48
Gardner, Randy, 167–68
Gershon, Stephen, 132–33
Gilligan, Carol, 39–42
Girl Scouts, 140
Girlish selfishness, 41
Global Family (company), 193
Global Mind Change (Harman), 179
Grafton, Sue, 81
Grief, 160–61
Griffin, W.E.B., 123–24
Gulf War, 107

H

Handless Maiden, The, 140–41
Harman, Willis, 179, 183
Hasselbein, Frances, 140
Hawken, Paul, 11
Here and now, awareness of, 36
Hitler, Adolph, 101
Holtby, Winifred, 87
HOPE (Honoring of People Everywhere),
194
House of Mirth, The (Wharton), 95
Human energy, containing and
orchestrating, 173
Humpty Dumpty rhyme, 1–2, 5, 178

I

Imagination, active, 200
Impatience, 28
In Memory of Old Jack (Berry), 10
In Midlife (Stein), 157
Incest and Human Love (Stein), xv, 31
Indifference, sense of, 64
Information
organizing, 81–94
sorting, 84–85
Initiator, role of, 171–72
Inner spirituality, 159
Inner work, 156–61
Insights, sudden big, 85
Inspirations from the field, 188–95
Instincts
following one's, 121–23
trusting, 29
Interdependence, shift to, 54–55
Interiority defined, 57
Intimate defined, 73
Intuition, 23

Invisible community, 69
Ishmael (Quinn), 131

J

Jordan, Judith V., 151
Jung, Carl, xii, 106, 109
Jungian depth psychology, xii, 96
Jungians, 105–6

K

K is for Killer (Grafton), 81
Keen, Sam, 2–3
Keller, Clare, 97
Kennedy, John F., 99, 199
Knowing Woman: A Feminine Psychology
  (Claremont de Castillejo), xv, 15, 61
Kohlberg, Lawrence, 39–40
Kubler-Ross, Elisabeth, 50

L

Language
  as a conceptual tool, 139
  problem of, 138–41
Leach-Bisson, Connie, 189
Leadership
  can take many forms, 195
  feminine, 111, 161, 178
Leadership Is an Art (DePree), 139–40
Lewis, Judie, 128–30
Lewis, Loida, 88–89
Life
  accepting cycles of, 45–59
  affirming, 31–43, 41
  attachment to, 39–43
  cycles of, 59
  economic, 6–9
  feminine affirmation of, 43
  supporting, 32
Lifestyle, view of one's, 183
Liminality, 157, 159
Living lightly, 185–88
Lover, feminine as, 175–78
Loving
  the dark, 56–59
  the earth, 177

M

McRae, Glen, 189
Madonna, Black, 200
Magic Eye, 9, 16
Maintenance
  of organizations, 89

and times of change, 88–93
Managers, strong, 22
Mang, Bob, 68, 127–28
Mariana, Sister, 176
Masculine; *See also* Female; Feminine;
    Women
  collaboration with the, 163–78
  consciousness, 10
  energy, 17, 161, 172–73
  radiant, 11
  world, 40–41
Masculine/feminine choreography, 167–
    70
Masculinity, focused consciousness, 5
Matter
  immersion in, 38
  natural deterioration of physical, 98
MBTI (Myers-Briggs Type Indicator),
    110
Means, living below one's, 187
Medical care system crisis, 69–70
Memories, Dreams, Reflections (Jung), xii
Memory of Old Jack, The (Berry), 127
Men, fairness in the public world of, 40
Miles, Margaret, 37–38, 93
Miller's daughter, 148–54
Millhone, Kinsey, 81, 84
Mind-sets, both-and and either-or, 23–26
Money, needing less, 186
Moon Hollow, 128–30
Moore, Thomas, 113
Moral development stages, 41–42
  acceptance of self, 42
  girlish selfishness, 41
  selflessness of women, 41
Mother bear, strategy, 120–21
Mother bear syndrome, 119–25
Mother Nature, fooling, 172
Mothering
  affirming individual worth, 117
  and being mothered, 113–25
  and the bitter emotional pain, 114
  in business, 115–19
  charge associated with, 114–16
  experiencing worth of others, 118
  false, 115–16
  good, 118
  keeping others out of harm's way, 117
  and nurturing, 125
  other people, 117
Muller, Robert, 179
Myers, Isabel Briggs, 110

N

Night, mystery of the, 58

O

Old Testament, 155
Olympics, Winter, 167
Omaha Beach, 100–103
On Men and Women (Bly, Woodman), 31
Orchestration and times of change, 88–93
Orchestrators, good, 92
Organizations, maintenance of, 89
Original Blessing (Fox), 10
Outcome, producing an, 90

P

Pains
    bitter emotional, 114
    experiencing labor, 48–49
Paradox, living with, 24
Passion
    feeling great, 177
    feminine, 37–39, 161
    finding real, 187
    St. Augustine's, 177
Past, primordial, 36
Patterns of change, 179–95
Peace and freedom, age of, 86
Peck, Scott, xv, 45, 49
Perfection, obsession with, 36
Persons, authentic values of, 73
Peters, Tom, 25
Physical reality, 35
Planetary survival and evolution, 52–53
Planting, companion, 17–18
Plenty, age of, 86
Poorer, simpler means, 183
Power
    acquiring and using, 75
    to trust, 169
Pregnant Virgin, The (Woodman), 145, 163
Presence, experiencing, 33–34
Primordial past, 36
Principle, feminine, 197
Psyche and Eros myth, 4–5, 82–84, 86,
    175–76
Psychic upheaval, 158–59
Psychology, Jungian depth, xii, 96

Q

Quinn, Daniel, 131

R

Racetrack, open, 197
Radiant masculine, 11
Rage, feminine, 119–25
Randolph girls basketball, 51–56
Realities
    experiencing, 33
    objective, 103
    physical and spiritual, 35
    subjective, 103–4
Reef, The (Wharton), 176
Reilly, Elaine, 21–23
Relationships
    building new standards, 198
    good thinking and good feelings, 109–
        10
    grace in, 170
    struggle with, 105
Rice, Sydney, 135–36
Risks, 56
Road Less Traveled, The (Peck), 45, 49

S

Sacred regard, 68, 70, 198
Scrimgeour, G. J., 96
Security, financial, 187
SEEDS: The Yearbook of Agriculture, 1961,
    86
Seeds, sorting, 82–86
Self, acceptance of, 42
Self-esteem
    increasing, 74–75
    strong individual, 118
Selfishness, girlish, 41
Selflessness of women, 41
Shaner, Hollie, 188–90
Silverman, Lois, 136–38
Simpler means poorer, 183
Skating, pairs figure, 167–68
Solstice, winter, 57–58
Sorrow, sweet, 96–100
Space
    creating good, 132–33
    defined, 164–65
    difficulty in creating good, 130–32
    linking tangible and intangible, 134–38
    sensibility about, 127–42
    simplifying one's living, 184–85
Spirit and matter split, 35–37
Spiritual and political worlds, 194
Spiritual reality, 35
Spirituality, inner, 159
Stabilization role, 165
Standards, building new, 198
Stein, Murray, 157
Stein, Robert, xv, 31, 34, 138
Stewardship, 172–73
Stone Center (Wellesley College), 151
Stress, perpetual, 98

Struggle with relationships, 105
Suffer, unwillingness to, 99
Survival, planetary, 52–53
Swimme, Brian, 58

T

The Coaching Company, 135
Thinking, clear, 104
Thunder Road (Barre, Vermont), 146
TLC Beatrice (Company), 88–89
Track, open, 146–48
Transition house for business, 99
Troy Motors (Michigan), 88
Trust
   power to, 169
   radical, 95–111
      in human beings, 105
      in individuals, 102–3
      and Omaha Beach, 100–103

U

Upheavals
   in business, 98
   psychic, 158–59
Urban/suburban culture, 183

V

Viner, Sophie, 176
Virgin defined, 169
von Franz, Marie Louise, 140–41, 148–50,
   152, 160

W

Wartime comradeship, 72
*Waste Management in Merger Conditions:
   Optimizing Systems* (American
   Hospital Association), 190
Wharton, Edith, 95, 176
Wholeness, interconnected, 39
Win/loss obsession, 53
Winter Olympics, 167
Winter Solstice
   celebrating the, 57–58
   and Christmas Eve, 58
Woman, anima, 163, 169
Woman's Growth In Connection (Jordan),
   151
Women; *See also* Female; Feminine;
   Masculine
   crying, 95–96
   leadership of, 111
   selflessness of, 41
   ways of working, 86–88
Woodman, Marion, xv, 31, 145, 163, 169–
   70, 173–74, 200
Work, inner, 156–59
World
   spiritual and political, 194
   understanding the workings of the,
   124–25

Y

Yin and yang, 168

Z

Zeus, 48